C0-AYK-129

CHRIST AND OURSELVES

ROGER HAZELTON

Christ and Ourselves

A CLUE TO CHRISTIAN LIFE TODAY

HARPER & ROW, PUBLISHERS
NEW YORK, EVANSTON, AND LONDON

FIRST EDITION

LIBRARY OF CONGRESS CATALOG CARD NUMBER: 65-15391

D-P

Contents

To consider Jesus Christ in everyone and in ourselves: Jesus Christ as father in his Father, Jesus Christ as brother among his brethren, Jesus Christ as poor among the poor, Jesus Christ as rich among the rich, Jesus Christ as teacher and priest among priests, Jesus Christ as sovereign among princes, etc. For by virtue of his glory as God he is all that is great; and by virtue of his mortal life he is all that is poor and abject. His purpose in assuming this wretched condition was to enable himself to be present in all persons and the model for all conditions of men.

Blaise Pascal, *Pensées*

Preface

Generally speaking, books on the subject of Jesus Christ are of two sorts. First, there is the theological treatise which is designed to make some contribution to the branch of Christian doctrine known as Christology. Such a book presents arguments in defense of a theory about Christ; it wrestles with inherited problems, takes sides on debated issues, and then puts forward a solution, whether this be an older position restated or a new approach justified. The second kind of book regarding Christ is devotional in nature and seeks to arouse or strengthen the fidelity of believers to their common Lord. It wishes to inspire rather than instruct; its language is suggestive, image-laden, ardent; and its object is not so much the solving of a problem as the evoking of a presence, through appeals addressed to the reader's heart and will.

This book may prove confusing or annoying to some readers because it refuses to choose between these alternatives. However, this is a risk that must be taken, because the alternatives themselves are unreal when it comes to speaking of Christ. After all, it is the Lord of inmost personal and corporate faith, the very anchor of our trust and hope in this world, about whom our sharpest and clearest thinking must be done. And not only is it faith which alone can give us a Christ to think about, but it is thought of a responsible and disciplined character which alone can structure and communicate the vital promptings of our faith in Christ. Hence in this book the purpose is that of understanding our faith in Christ, neither taking faith for granted altogether nor presuming that it can be created at the end of a chain of reasoning, but insisting that ardor and accuracy, loyalty and clarity need each other and must stand together. This is always true where Christian matters are being considered, and nowhere is it more true than in reflecting upon the meaning of Jesus Christ.

Sooner or later every theologian must take up the task of saying what he believes regarding Christ, though he may certainly be pardoned if he does so a bit hesitantly, as this is already a much traveled path beset with many dangers to both mind and spirit. The possibilities of misunderstanding and of being misunderstood are great indeed. Nevertheless, this risky journey of faithful thought has to be made, if only because the theologian finds himself asking who he is and why he thinks at all. To be a Christian, as St. Augustine wrote, is to belong to Christ; and it follows that to do one's thinking as a Christian will require that every thought, in St. Paul's words, be brought into captivity to Christ.

Surely the Apostle here sets forth the underlying motive of all theology and especially all Christological reflection; yet how quickly his injunction is forgotten once the theologian gets down to work! Instead of becoming captivated by the Christ, theology has persisted in trying to capture him within its own formulations. Thus creeds originally voiced in awesome gratitude, vibrant with mystery, have acquired in later times the semblance of a sacrosanct finality from which almost all margins of wonder are removed. Rightness of belief has been made the function of correctness of statement concerning Christ. It is an old and familiar story, the way in which theology has substituted the verbal for the real, a confining for a liberating truth.

Is this inveterate tendency also an inevitable one? In this book we shall try to show that it is not. Our aim will be to take a fresh look at the meaning of Christ for our own time and place, not by reshuffling ancient categories or rephrasing knotty problems, but by following out some Christological clues as they may be seen to bear upon urgent Christian concerns. We shall approach the age-old question of who Christ is and what he does not by definition or description so much as by implication and suggestion.

Among the clues which might be chosen to throw light upon our situation as Christian men and women living in the world today, one commends itself as most reliable and pertinent. This is the theme of God's involvement, his incognito, within faith's own manner of life. We shall be tracing out this theme in such fields of Christian questioning and acting as the form and function of the Church, the patterns of ministry and worship, the dialogue with the world. Also it will be necessary to take our bearings from time to time with reference to still larger and more strictly theological concerns, like the relationship of Christ to God and to his Holy Spirit.

By this means, it is earnestly hoped, old truth can presently come alive, and our thought may once again be brought more fully into captivity to Christ.

A closing word of personal acknowledgment is now in order. The chapters that follow have taken shape in connection with three groups of lectures which I have had the honor to deliver. Accordingly I wish to express my gratitude to all those who made arrangements, helped by comment and suggestion, and encouraged the reworking of these lectures with a view to publication. Especially I thank most heartily President Gene Bartlett for his invitation and hospitality when the Dahlberg Lectures were given at Colgate-Rochester Divinity School; President Robert Fauth of Eden Theological Seminary for friendly assistance in planning the Alumni Lectures there; and Dean Masashi Takahashi and Professor

Masao Takenaka for their very gracious reception at Doshisha University in Kyoto, Japan, where I had the privilege of lecturing in October, 1964.

ROGER HAZELTON

The Graduate School of Theology
Oberlin College
Oberlin, Ohio

CHRIST AND OURSELVES

CHAPTER I

Christ—and God

1

Today, for more people than one likes to admit, Christian or not, the question about God greatly overshadows any questions we may ask about Christ. So true is this that no one can presume to give real answers to the latter sort of question if he has not at least listened intently to the former. There is good reason for worrying about the integrity of a "Church theology" which seems so preoccupied with making claims for Christ that it evades, or holds at bay, the prior question about God. It is as if we were attempting, unconsciously perhaps, to cover up the root-anxiety of our age by going through the motions of reiteration and reassurance, by putting a high premium upon Christ as a kind of God-substitute.

But the question about God will not be managed or bypassed so easily, for it intrudes upon our shaky security with clamant frequency. Even a passing acquaintance with contemporary literature and other art forms reveals unmistakably that this *is* the prior question, not perhaps in the sense that it must be settled first but in the sense that it has to be asked and heard first, if the Church's familiar utterances regarding Jesus Christ are going to have real meaning. And while it is certainly true that the question about God is often not so much an outright interrogation as it is a kind of uneasy disturbance, vaguely defined yet keenly felt, it does need answering even if such answers cannot be found conveniently in the back of the Christian book. Can we in all honesty continue talking about Christ without realizing that our ancestors' faith in anything remotely resembling Deity is drastically missing among us? Such talk is naturally more than suspect if it goes on in an atmosphere sealed off from the tang and bite of present-day experience, with its aching void where belief in God used to be.

Even if Christ is indeed remembered and known still, as John Knox says, within the community of Christian faith, just what he has to do with God, or God with him, is very far from being understood at all decisively or surely. When divinity is such an unknown quantity it is not particularly helpful to call Christ divine. It is hardly a secret that our life today is far less confident of God than the proliferation of religious activities and agencies would appear to suggest. The world as we have come to know it is a "God-haunted house." Most of us in fact have become habituated to getting along without God, to living from day to day as if God were silent and absent from our engagements and endeavors. That Christ is still spoken of and cherished in the institutions which bear his name ought not to mislead anyone for a moment into thinking that belief in God comes easily or naturally to us any longer. The truth is that it does not.

Men make response to this haunting absence of God in diffierent ways. One characteristic and enthusiastic form of response is that suggested by the phrase "Christianity without religion." On these terms religion means taking part in those organized structures and programs which go by the name of "church" in our culture. We scan what Peter Berger calls "the establishment," trying to discover the marks of God at work in it; and since such signs are very hard to come by, we end by repudiating all institutional involvement in the name of

Christ. It is felt that if we could attain a personal depth of faith without merely getting encumbered in the snares of the established Christain order, then we would have made an authentic response to the gospel. If God is obviously lacking in the organizations which claim to act and speak for him, then are we not more radically obedient to God in abandoning them to their own devices?

That some of us should become wearied by the noise of solemn assemblies is altogether healthy and right. The proponents of a religionless Christianity do have a valid point to make and they deserve a sympathetic hearing. Too much of what passes for religion at the moment is obviously conformist, cliché-ridden, spineless when confronted by revolutionary social change—and the charges can be indefinitely extended. A profound transvaluation of the Church's scheme of values is plainly overdue. But such a critical backlash, however salutary, will not assuage, much less remove, the general lack of faith in the God of our fathers at the center of life.

What is actually happening here? It is plain that one may be for God and at the same time against religion. But is it not equally plain that by transferring the center of attention from the question about God to that of what constitutes a genuine faith, we do not dispose of the former question but only make it more persistent and acute? Christianity without religion may be an appealing, viable option for some; but faith without God is only the latest form of the absurd.

A more direct, head-on attempt to cope with the question about God is that recently brought to popular focus by Bishop J. A. T. Robinson in his widely discussed book *Honest to God.* Our trouble, he insists, is that we have been looking for God in the wrong places; God is not to be found either "up there" or "out there," as former generations thought. Science has utterly disabused us of these older notions of divine transcendence, although this word has evidently been long in reaching many otherwise modern minds.

It is now much more to the point, says Bishop Robinson, that we should use the word "God" to mean "the infinite and inexhaustible depth and ground of all being"—this phrase he borrows from Paul Tillich—if theology is to make real contact with the present world. And he maintains, following Dietrich Bonhoeffer, that ours is actually a Godless world, for God has ceased to be necessary to guarantee religious enterprises, to justify laws or customs, or to underwrite our morals. Such a God, let's face it, is simply not around any more. The old myths have lost their wonted charm and power over us. Men and women in a "world come of age" should acknowledge this fact, no matter how distressing it may prove to be.

Bishop Robinson's viewpoint is commendable in taking us to the heart of the question about God, but what must be asked is whether "depth" is to be preferred to "height" as a metaphorical way of indicating the divine. Let it be fully granted, with Robinson, that Christian faith does not have to be interpreted by means of mythical and supernatural language that is, to put it kindly, anachronistic. Yet it is also the case that any language about God, whether up-to-date or old-fashioned, will have to rely on creaturely imagery of some sort, drawn from the stuff of our experience, since this is all we have. What Bishop Robinson is really objecting to in his book is not the use of one dimension over against another, but the ingrained tendency to suppose that words signaling God can be taken seriously only if they are taken literally too. In this objection we must join him. Let it be clear, however, that the revisions he proposes are not less symbolic but only differently so, no matter how much more congenial or persuasive they are.

There is an even more fundamental question to be asked about this brave attempt. Bishop Robinson and others have a great deal to say about the "God-shaped blank" within the consciousness of modern man; but is this actually displaced or overcome by what must frankly be termed a blank-shaped God? Even Paul Tillich, it is worth noting, has had some second thoughts about his emphasis upon "depth." The point which needs to be made here is that theological "depth" bears an uncomfortably close resemblance to the "abyss" of nihilistic, atheistic interpretations of human existence. The Christian faith is surely not a stranger to real doubt, but it can scarcely thrive except in response to actual intimations of God's power and presence within the experienced world itself. "I had fainted," said the Psalmist, "unless I had believed to see the goodness of the Lord in the land of the living." That is always and unmistakably true.

Let it be quickly added that the Psalmist's affirmation does not mean giving up divine transcendence altogether. It does not make God out to be a "piece of the world," in Gerhard Ebeling's phrase. For if God were a part of this interpretable world he could not at the same time serve as any kind of principle for interpreting it by the terms and norms of faith. A world interpreted by reference to God is not a world of which God can be a part. And yet, when all is said, our faith does need for its awakening and nourishment some genuine signs or tokens of a working in the world that is both good and great enough to be called divine. One does not have to be inclined toward pantheism or gnosticism, new style, to grant the force of this point. Faith may be indeed, as Søren Kierkegaard wrote, a "leap," but it is not a leap in the dark, at least not altogether. Faith does not, cannot, emerge in a complete vacuum. It is not a merely arbitrary reading of the admitted ambiguities of history and of nature ("Some call it nothingness, and others call it God"). Any sort of faith deserving the name must have its own sufficient occasion and stimulus.

Recognizing the truth of this, we are led to put a question to the thought of Dietrich Bonhoeffer. When he writes that we must do without God in the world and yet must look for Christ "at the center of life," what does he actually mean to be saying? That we should give up looking for God in the sky or beyond outer space is certainly true enough, and most of us have wisely ceased to do so. Also it is evident that our kind of world is not going about its business as if it needed the hypothesis of God, and this must be given due importance as the fact it is. And yet, says Bonhoeffer, it is at the center of life that Christ must be searched out. What is this if not the very milieu where man and nature meet, where events transpire and experiences occur, and which both conditions and provokes our responses? Is this not the same world in which we have been told that we must do without God?

It is, of course, but then we have a problem, as the saying goes. Is it Bonhoeffer's point that since God is missing from the world we must restrict ourselves to looking for Christ there? Hardly, because he believes and states his belief that Christ himself is the revelation of God, but a strangely hidden and enigmatic one. The only way in which this difficulty can be understood is with the help of the incognito, God's self-disclosure through his self-concealment. Succeeding chapters in this book will return often to this theme.

However our initial observation stands, that for our troubled age the question about God takes precedence over the one concerning Christ. Enough has already been said to show that these two questions cannot be faced or resolved in separation from each other. What matters most is where we put our weight, what sort of answer we are expecting. Our own period in history is not simply post-Christian, as it is often termed, but residually and reminiscently Christian. Thus the God who is widely doubted or denied is by no means deity-in-general but he whom centuries of Christian piety and practice have identified as the Father of our Lord Jesus Christ. No issue can be firmly joined, and no effective ground rules can be established, in the growing dialogue of belief with unbelief unless this significant fact is seen for what it is.

Since, then, the question about God is raised for us most

often in its Christian form, especially in the cultural West but increasingly throughout the East as well, it either assumes or implies the question about Christ too. Accordingly our thinking will now turn toward the impact and interpenetration of these two related questions upon one another.

2

How "in the land of the living" are we to take up again the search for God? Must we forever be confronted only by absence and silence where God is concerned? Certainly the old "proofs" for God which argued from the order and constancy of nature have lost their hold upon the present-day mind. Or can it be maintained with reasonable cogency and persuasiveness that we are not utterly without God in the world? The question here is whether there are any signs of "the goodness of the Lord" which have what might be called evidential value.

One thing is fairly clear at the outset. If any such vision is to be vouchsafed to men and women of our own time, it will not come as self-evident or with compelling, doubt-dispelling force. We shall not be able, like our fathers in the faith, to recognize God in his glorious majesty, surrounded by all the well-known marks of divinity. Where in a world such as ours are we to look for those assurances of omniscience, omnipresence, and omnipotence which have been made familiar by centuries of Christian teaching and worshiping? We may sing "God is the ruler yet," but our behavior both inside and outside the precincts of the church gives the lie to our profession. We may go on speaking of cosmic triumph already established over human guilt and death; but neither in our attitudes toward the offender nor in our funeral and burial practices do we take such speaking seriously. Many other indications might be given to demonstrate with quite impressive finality that belief in a God who reveals himself directly and powerfully is basically foreign to us, if not in our rituals then surely in our normal experience and conduct as contemporary men and women.

No, the intimations of God afforded by our kind of world are not those positive, unambiguous "evidences" which seemed to abound in earlier ages when, as Matthew Arnold wrote, "the sea of faith was at the full." Traditional talk about a being who is supposed to preside over the affairs of men, whose prerogatives are properly described in the images of authority and sovereignty may of course persist for a long time in the Church and elsewhere. But the well of conviction out of which these words and symbols arise is slowly, surely drying up. "Something serious has happened," Karl Jaspers says. It has indeed.

Any glimpse of God made possible in our world must come through other channels and with a different kind of reverberation. It must come instead, if it is to come at all, through a sobering vision of God's weakness, vulnerability, and humiliation. "Only a suffering God can help," in the frequently cited words of Bonhoeffer, because only such a God makes sense of the kind of world in which conventional Christian assurance about divine authority and victory finds no echo in our experience or reason. That is the plain, hard truth.

But is this not precisely to affirm that true knowledge of God comes *sub specie Christi* if it is to come to us at all? Under the form of Christ, God is revealed just by virtue of his hiddenness; he bears, so to speak, a negative witness to himself. He flashes no credentials of divinity. He does not announce his own arrival on the human scene or give advance proofs of his real identity. He fulfills our expectations by transforming them completely. This is the true import of what we Christians believe to be the Incarnation, as of the redemption of the world which is, according to our faith, God's inner, final purpose.

This judgment is borne out by even a cursory acquaintance

with the renaissance of faith in a God who works incognito and who speaks off the record—a renaissance emphatically illustrated in the contemporary arts. When, for example, we read the novels of Graham Greene or François Mauriac we find them setting forth the action of God within human situations in just this ambiguous and secret manner. In their portrayal God imparts himself not through the expected channels of customary religious commitment so much as through a surprising, shaking kind of hiddenness, using what Tillich calls the "broken symbols" of secularity, even of profanity, to make himself known. In stories like these God manages to convey his healing, recreating grace by very earthen vessels, by renegade priests or sullen prostitutes, just as in Rouault's paintings the clown becomes an unmistakable type of Christ.

What is being brought home to us in this contemporary Christian art is the truth that "Grace is insidious, it twists and turns and is full of surprises," as Charles Péguy wrote more than a generation ago. God's characteristic way of acting within and upon human life is through self-concealment, self-abandonment. On these terms, the Incarnation and the redemption it effects must be understood as something other than the pinpointing or highlighting of God in human history. Rather, what holds our attention in these art-forms is God getting himself lost in history, yielding up his supernatural and superhuman attributes precisely in order to identify himself with us at the profoundest level possible.

And is this not the very meaning of the Christian gospel? Here too God is believed to reveal himself within the forms of hiddenness. It is as one "crossed for the sins of the world," in Joseph Hardy Neesima's words, that he makes known his will, the avenue to his Kingdom, and his claim upon our obedience. For if God were to stand clear to faith in some bare, unhidden fashion he would simply not be revealing *himself*. No, in order to do this he becomes one with me in my own kind of life, making its web of circumstance his own, taking his chances so to speak with all its obscurities and obstacles. Thus, and only thus, do I come to know him as he truly is.

Theologians have been on the whole more hesitant than writers and artists in drawing out these implications of the gospel. Being naturally very zealous to preserve what seems to them the Godhood of God, theologians tend to throw so many provisos in the path of Christian thought that the truth of the gospel dies "the death of a thousand qualifications." So Karl Barth speaks guardedly, in time-honored fashion to be sure, of God "assuming" manhood in Jesus Christ; and Tillich takes great care to stress the "symbolic" element in his view of Christ. But the event of Christ does not mean that God simply adds manhood to what is already his own nature, or that he reflects himself, however flawlessly, in a human mirror. It means involvement, full incarnate identification with our very humanness, or the gospel itself is missing from our theology. This point must be underscored repeatedly in the course of theological development, and has a special urgency at the present time.

For the most part contemporary theologians are wary of the Pauline teaching of the *kenosis* or self-emptying of God; they prefer to follow safer theological traditions in striking a nice balance between divinity and humanity when interpreting the meaning of Christ, while indicating the dangers bound up in saying that God surrenders what is rightfully his own nature when he enters savingly into human existence. In this vein Barth wants it distinctly understood that in taking humanity upon himself in Christ God does this "without ceasing to be God"—as if St. Paul or his interpreters had ever claimed the opposite. So too in Tillich's theology it is laid down that all statements about God, including those made in Christian worship and doctrine, are "symbolic" except the statement that God is "being itself"—as if this designation alone could escape the ills that mortal speech is heir to whenever God is in question.

But God does not need our theological permission or verbal protection in order to be God. Tillich and Barth are well aware of this, of course; but it is a great temptation to any theologian to want to have the last, most definitive word to say about God. It is no repudiation of the durable, brilliant achievements of the theology of Barth and Tillich if we choose to insist, as we must, that God in Christ is not chary of his Godhood and that his becoming one with us in manhood is, of all his mighty acts, the one that is most revealing of his inmost will and purpose.

Must not Christian theology, then, still try to find better ways of saying that God's being is indeed his being-for-others, that he discloses who he is by the tragic obscurity of the cross? Whatever may be the logical or historical outcome of such efforts, they must at least keep faith with the truth of the gospel itself. It is with this important need in mind that we are focusing in these chapters upon the theme of God's incognito as we encounter it in Christ and in the world where Christian living must be done.

A question may be forming at this point within the minds of some, however. Is not the incognito theme merely the reiteration of what theologians know as the Christological paradox, and if so, what can it add by way of basic understanding to the classic statements of Church creeds and councils in the ancient world? The question is a good one and deserves a reply. Theologians have indeed, following the formula of Chalcedon, tended to force their thinking about Christ into the mold of orthodox, deliberate self-contradiction, and so defined Christ as at once "very God" and "very man." It is as if you and I already know what Godhood and manhood are and now have only to combine them in a new and paradoxical dimension.

But we do not know what Godhood is; in fact, it is the axiom of all theology that God is infinite and so incomprehensible. And neither do we know very well what manhood is; the mystery of being human is forever with us and must be acknowledged, not verbalized away, in Christian thought. Hence the problem for Christology is not that of combining two already known "natures" within a single paradoxical conception. When a theologian says "God-man-hood" with respect to Jesus Christ, he has not solved his difficulty but only located it.

The formula of Chalcedon, to which theologians look back with workmanlike respect, can probably not be improved upon as a protection against heresy. According to it, there is to be neither division nor confusion, neither separation nor identity between the human and divine "natures" of Christ. This is all very well, provided that one is sure of what these "natures" mean, and obviously the framers of this formula had far more confidence in this regard than we can claim today. But Chalcedon, however indispensable in its negative way, is scarcely capable of stimulating Christological reflection of a sort which leads us to say that about Jesus Christ which needs saying, terribly and wonderfully, in our own time and place. What Chalcedon does is to protect the mystery of Christ, by giving necessary warning that whatever is said about Christ, more remains to be said. But it should not be used to keep theology in bondage to any paradoxical strait-jacket; it should, rather, be allowed to encourage, amplify, and unsettle our thought concerning Christ, as the working principle of contrasting and correcting truth.

What, really, is meant by the term "paradox"? Ever since Kierkegaard's striking identification of God-in-Christ with "the Paradox," and with its immense influence upon recent theology, this question has become urgent. A paradox, in its original sense, is something which goes beyond or passes belief. It does not refer to the merely incredible or absurb, but to that which is more and not less than believable. In short, a paradox always signals mystery. It is not the perfect, certainly not the only form for setting forth what is mysterious, but it is especially valuable in alerting us to the very limited capacities of words and thoughts in expressing whatever is insistently real. In common speech, analogy and metaphor also fulfill this function. But when a paradox is ventured, this amounts to saying that we are at our wits' end and know it.[1]

What is highly important, in speaking theologically about Christ, is that the mystery of God acting in him should be permitted to break through what is said about him; indeed, the most adequate utterance is precisely that which best conveys its own inadequacy to this task. Touching the mystery of God-in-Christ we have to believe because we cannot know. The use of paradox in setting forth this mystery may be helpful at many points, provided that the paradox is not taken as synonymous with the mystery itself. In fact, we may say that while expressions of the truth about Christ will doubtless have a paradoxical edge, such truth ought not to be regarded as equivalent to paradox alone. Always in theology we have to be on guard against substituting what is only a guard rail for the very roadway of our thought, which must remain free and open toward the mystery of Christ.

3

Turning now in a different direction, have we any clues from the sayings of Jesus as to what he himself believed about his relationship with God? If such clues were forthcoming, then Christian theology could not afford to neglect them, since they would enable us, to some degree at least, to fill out and correct our own thinking about Christ by reference to Jesus' thought concerning himself.

However, as everyone is aware, more than a century of critical biblical scholarship has made us very wary of proceeding in this direction. We have learned that it is simply not

[1] I have treated this matter more thoroughly, in a passage which may still hold some interest, in my book *Renewing the Mind* (New York: The Macmillan Company, 1949), pp. 137-142.

possible to isolate the "Jesus of history" from the "Christ of faith," for the very good reason that it is faith itself which does the writing of the New Testament. Therefore, the authenticity of any particular saying must be patiently, carefully established by following closely the rules of textual and historical criticism, and even then it cannot in many instances be fully guaranteed. To take but one example, the Fourth Gospel, in which Jesus is pictured as talking most about himself (one of the problems in continuous debate is that of where quotations end), is also that furthest removed in time from the events and words which it records.

In studying the Gospels, then, theologians must depend upon the current findings of critical scholars. Particularly is this so when considering the names or titles given to Jesus in the New Testament writings, and most of all those designations which Jesus is reported to apply to himself.[2] It is important to Christology, for instance, to know whether "Messiah" is a term expressing status and position vis-à-vis God, or only function and task. Yet theological inquiry will regard this as chiefly a matter of emphasis in either case, as it is clearly meaningless to speak of a duty which is not also an office, or of responsibility apart from authority. The elements of human expectation and divine appointment which enter into the term "Messiah" likewise must be analyzed with care, but also comprehensively related to each other in the total biblical conception.

One point on which there seems to be an impressive critical consensus is that the earliest traditions include Jesus' description of himself as "Son of man" and as the son of his "heavenly Father." What interests us most as theologians, of course, is the actual meaning which these titles may have had for Jesus and now should have for us. In his treatment of the

[2] See especially Vincent Taylor, *The Names of Jesus* (London: Macmillan & Company, 1953); Oscar Cullmann, *Christology in the New Testament* (Philadelphia: The Westminster Press, 1954).

former term, after reviewing some of the scholarly literature, Ethelbert Stauffer comments that "Son of man" is "just about the most pretentious piece of self-description that any man in the ancient East could possibly have used!"[3] This is a decided reversal of the direction laid down by liberal scholars of a generation ago who found in this title an assurance of the fact that Jesus wished to be regarded only as a man among men. But the earliest Gospel, Mark, identifies the celestial ruler of the apocalyptic tradition with the suffering servant of the prophetic tradition. His servanthood is for Mark the very proof that God is incognito in him and that the Son of man's true glory will one day be fully revealed for what it truly is.

Nor is it otherwise with Jesus' evident description of himself in terms of a filial relationship to his Father in heaven. While he might at first be expected to stress his exalted, unique nature, it turns out instead that he is pointing here toward the necessity of his obedience and dependence upon God. To be the son of God means, like all sonship, both kinship and separation. Yet when Jesus so refers to himself, although there is sometimes the hint of a secret understanding or preincarnate oneness with God, his characteristic and repeated emphasis is upon what ancient theologians called his "subordination" evidenced in prayer, trust, and not least in the struggle of his own will against that of his Father.

At all events we do not find in such titles as these any thoroughgoing equivalents for the "very God" and "very man" of later doctrinal development. A mysterious relationship is certainly disclosed, but this is scarcely to be made synonymous with the familiar Christological paradox. Through Jesus' self-understanding as recorded in the Gospels, we are confronted with something both more and less problematical than an abstract antithesis of "natures" or "substances." We have more of a problem because, instead of

[3] *New Testament Theology* (New York: The Macmillan Company, 1955), p. 108.

outright paradox, we are presented with a whole complex series of events, decisions, and sayings that are not foregone conclusions but unfinished business, as it were, on the divine agenda. But it is also less problematic, in the sense that the New Testament neither asks nor answers the question about who Christ is in the traditional Nicene or Chalcedonian manner.

If paradox we must have, it is that of the God who alone can save man, moving to do so by and through an undeniably human life. Yes, the real paradox, or mystery-alert, for Christology is that of one who "is in *humility* the highest," as Barth puts it. The Christological "problem" is closely linked with that of Christian discipleship itself—that of finding life by losing it, of exaltation by the very means of humility, of mastery through servanthood. Hence, to quote Barth again, "The death on the cross is indeed only the unfolding of the incarnation."[4] If this be called a paradox, then it must also be admitted that it is paradox of a most unusual, thought-compelling and not thought-confining kind.

And furthermore, if the Gospel is true, as it is believed to be, the story of what God is doing in Jesus Christ is a paradox no longer. Not that all contradictions are thereby removed from our thinking in faith about Christ; far from it. Nor is it claimed here that a completely nonparadoxical interpretation of his person and his work can be presented for the edification of the present Christian generation; not at all. The meaning of Christ for Christians is not something which submits to smooth generalization and the kind of packaged statement in which we are all too prone to try to wrap up our beliefs. And yet, because the Church's apprehension of the Christ is always outrunning our comprehension of his meaning, we must not go on forever refining and sharpening the ancient forms of paradox, merely translating it into what we are pleased to

[4] *The Epistle to the Philippians* (Richmond, Va.: John Knox Press, 1962), p. 62.

call fresh language, and updating it into the terms of whatever theology or metaphysics happens to be fashionable. The meaning of Christ *is* the mystery of his relationship to God; and this, if you will pardon the expression, is para-paradoxical, that is, it both makes paradoxes necessary and refuses to be exhausted within them.

But let us return to Jesus' words about himself. What meaning does he seem to make out of his own mystery? When we discover Jesus speaking about his relationship with God his Father, we do not hear the voice which speaks of likeness to God in him so much as we hear the voice that speaks of likeness to him in God. This distinction is by no means as clever or specious as it may appear. Even the statement, "He who has seen me has seen the Father," as reported in the Fourth Gospel, is suggestive on this score. It does not have to be understood as an apodictic proposition in which Christ is making unique, divine claims for himself, in contradiction to the obvious fact that he is also a man among men. We grasp its meaning better, more profoundly, if we see it as the expression of the truth that Jesus Christ is transparent to the very being and intent of God. Whatever the stress of the church in later ages, Jesus' own stress is clearly upon the fact not that he is like God, but that God is like him.

How important this stress is can be seen if we contrast it, as we must, with some subsequent developments in Christian theological history. Speaking quite generally, it may be said that once the New Testament canon is closed, the images and titles of Christ are transformed into categories that are more or less philosophical and even metaphysical in character. We must admit, it is true, that as soon as Christ was preached as Lord to the Greek mind, the problem of his being or nature with reference to God was unavoidably raised. As a result Christology has gone through a whole series of complicated philosophical mutations—in which, incidentally, as Oscar Cullmann reminds us, the interpretation of Christ's person and work was subjected to the question of his proper "substance." Down into the present time these successive transformations into the dominant patterns of philosophy have gone on in theology. The question for us, perhaps even more acutely than for earlier generations, is whether despite this long history an authentic biblical accent can be recovered. Can we, without discounting or attempting to discredit real issues of a chiefly philosophical sort, renew our Christological reflection at its biblical source? Can we, in short, encounter Christ in our thought, with an eye to Scripture rather than Chalcedon, and not remain theologically impervious to what he has to tell us regarding himself?

4

Quite recently, in pondering the answer to these questions, I came by chance upon an intriguing little book by François Mauriac entitled *The Son of Man*. It is as far from being a professional theological treatment of this theme as could well be imagined. Instead, this gifted Roman Catholic layman presents a free-wheeling, ruminative monologue upon the meaning which Christ holds for him. On the first page of the book is a sentence which, as Denis de Rougemont might say, is a trap for meditation. It is this: "God is not only a Father; He is also an Eternal Child."

What makes this cryptic, disarmingly casual observation so arresting? Its undeniable ring of truth comes, I believe, from the almost jaunty manner in which it brushes aside schools and creeds to get to the heart of the matter Christologically. Here Mauriac is saying not that Christ is to be understood in terms of God so much as that God must be understood by means of Christ. Yet he is clearly orthodox in his view; Sonship, as well as Fatherhood, belongs to God.

For the most part, recent biblical theology, as it is called, has been moving in quite an opposite direction. Terms like

"Christocentric" and "Christomonism" have had to be invented to describe the tendency. It has seemed all-important to delineate "faith's picture of the Christ" through passing in review a curiously static list of scriptural phrases and titles. And there, all too often, the matter has been allowed to stand. At times, in reading biblical theology, it almost seems that lexicography has usurped the rightful place of constructive theology in thinking about Christ. It would appear that "hermeneutics" is king, having driven out what used to be known as "substance of doctrine."

Principles of interpretation we must surely have, drawn from the Bible although not restricted to it. But if Christology is central to the theological enterprise, as it assuredly is, then it must be inquired what makes it central. And the answer that needs to be given is that if Christ is indeed central to our understanding of God, it is because God is basic to our understanding of Christ. (I have often been dismayed at the confusion of what is *basic* with what is *central* in current theological writing and discussion.) Does not the New Testament itself place the characteristic emphasis here, by insisting that matters of faith are also matters of truth? Indeed, it never seems to lose sight of the priority of God. Thus we read, "God was in Christ reconciling the world . . ." and "God so loved the world that he gave. . . ." When this priority is laid aside we do not have Christology at all.

Mauriac's sentence about the eternal childhood of God, in addition to remaining faithful to this priority, also is valuable in stressing weakness and vulnerability in God as Christians understand and respond to him. The father-image, taken by itself, is not adequate for conveying the full truth of the Gospel. If God is only an authority-figure blown up to cosmic proportions, as some not too cultured despisers of Christianity have charged, then he is simply not the Father of our Lord Jesus Christ. We do not tack on the concrete, historical details of human servanthood to the supposed divine attributes of pre-eminence and sovereignty as a kind of Christian afterthought or amplification. Not at all; for unlike other lofty monotheisms our faith takes its stand upon the truth that God does not keep to himself but becomes implicated with us, lives our life and dies our death, in order to redeem us.

How do we know in faith that God *is* God? By virtue of the fact that his Word became flesh and dwelt among us full of grace and truth. That is to say, through Jesus Christ our Lord. We take his Incarnation seriously, not as the manifestation of an otherwise hidden God, nor as the realization of a hitherto unknown potentiality in God, but as the purposeful disclosure of God's very heart and being. What is divine in God, if we may put it so, is nothing other than his being-for-us which Christians call by the word "love." To say, then, "God in Christ" does not amount to saying "God plus Christ." Rather, the only God we know is the enmanned God who makes our human flesh his cradle and his cross. It is exactly his humble presence in our midst which is the sign and the seal of his power over us.

Hence it becomes the actual proof of God that he should take our condition upon himself, that in Christ he should make himself sin, as St. Paul does not hesitate to declare. In Christ, through whom we have our access to the Father, God as the Son shares our griefs and bears our guilt, a needy human being all the way. Flesh and blood alone do not, cannot, achieve this miracle of radically brotherly love. Only God can do so.

Childhood, furthermore, implies not only humble weakness but also newness and innocence. Mauriac's statement is therefore suggestive in yet another way. God who makes all things new, who sums up all creation under a new head, is he to whom purity belongs in an eminent, unique sense. Yet purity in God, as disclosed by Christ, is surely no antiseptic attribute. It does not signify that God is wholly uncontaminated by the sin that soils our lives, or that in Christ he is something less than completely human. We come much closer to the right approach in William Blake's *Songs of Innocence* or in Gerard Manley Hopkins' evocation of "a dearest freshness deep down things."

It is appropriate to speak of the innocence of God because this is so large a part of what the atonement means. The guilt Christ bore was not his own but others', and his solidarity with man was through and through vicarious and representative, not merely a cross-section of the whole *massa perditionis,* as St. Augustine termed humanity. "Sinlessness" is probably far too pale and too exclusively moral a term to express this. What theology requires is a term which conveys the truth, not that God is untouched or unsullied by our sin, but that he overcomes it, crowds it out, by the creative energies of his pure Spirit. "It is innocence that is full and experience that is empty", says Péguy, adding that this "unique grace" is chiefly the mark of the little child.[5]

In his book Mauriac is evidently circling about the same truth: "But the Infant God naked upon the straw is the only one who is really all-powerful. . . . upon the straw of Bethlehem He is still 'He who is'; not the Child-God but the God who has become a Child—the God-Child."[6] This is yet another way of stating that as seen and met in Christ, God is the power of new being, of being new. The message of Christmas is one with that of Good Friday and Easter. Incarnation and atonement together constitute the truth of the gospel.

Accordingly, it should not strike us as surprising that the life "in Christ" is described in similar language. To become as little children is the New Testament's way of setting forth the personal requirement for entering into the kingdom of God, that is, his realm and reign in earthly human living and beyond. In Jesus' own teaching there is certainly no romanti-

[5] *God Speaks* (New York: Pantheon Books, 1945), pp. 38-41.

[6] *The Son of Man,* trans. Bernard Murchland (Cleveland: World Publishing Company, 1960), pp. 19, 21.

cized picture of childhood as the age of utter innocence, yet all the same the child is often used to voice the wonder, freshness, and open dependence of faith in relation to the God disclosed in Christ.

These are but a few of the materials for Christological reflection suggested by Mauriac's pregnant sentence. My own conviction, for whatever it is worth, is that considerations such as these may be useful in getting Christology off the dead center where it now appears to stand. In the chapters that follow, however, we shall not be engaged in trying to prove the truth of this assertion, but in a Christological exploration of the terrain of Christain faith and life. At times we shall be very much on our own, at others we shall be expounding some traditional doctrines. But at all times we shall keep in view the towering, indispensable conviction that God is like Jesus Christ, so that whoever truly sees him sees his Father too.

In the following chapters of this book we shall be using this conviction as a clue for understanding various facets and concerns of Christian faith and life today. One premise of our exploration is that Jesus Christ is not an isolated phenomenon awaiting theological anaylsis, but God's incognito or "open secret" very much involved and at work in our midst. This theme will be traced out with more fullness at some points than at others, but it will always be standing in the background. If it were to become too explicit or finely polished, then we would simply not be keeping faith with the theme itself.

Another premise is that matters of Christian living need to be interpreted according to Christ. We shall better understand what we are about in Church and world if the connection with God's loving deed in Jesus can be seen for what it Christianly is. The meaning of the mystery in which we are caught up is that of being "hid with Christ in God."

CHAPTER II

Christ and the Church

The subject of this chapter is entirely natural and expected, perhaps too much so. If a theologian undertakes to examine the relationship between the Church and Christ, his examination is supposed to yield assurance that this relationship is intimate, essential, and integral to the being of the Church. Since it has become an axiom of our theological epoch that every theologian necessarily speaks for the Church and wholly within faith, it is taken for granted that the closest possible linkage of the Church with its Lord will be established, that communion and continuity with him must be expounded as the order of the day.

And this has in fact happened to a very large degree. Perhaps no sector of contemporary theological inquiry is as smug or self-assured as that which deals with the Lordship of Christ in relation to the community which bears his name. However, there is something much too familiar in the typical treatment of this matter which gives an honest theologian pause. Recalling Dostoevsky's Grand Inquisitor and Nietzsche's Zarathustra, he is obliged to stress the discontinuity and disobedience of the Church. He finds it necessary to account for the fact that we may betray our Lord as well as live in faithful discipleship to him within the Church.

A robust, unbiased theology will take upon itself the task

of interpreting the Church in terms of its treasons no less than its loyalties, even though this may shatter Christian complacency or call radically into question the "blest communion, fellowship divine." And it is precisely on behalf of Christ's own Lordship that this must be done, and therefore also for the sake of the Church itself.

1

The Church of Christ is neither a simple nor a single thing. Especially in an ecumenical era like the present, we cannot even speak of it, or begin to discuss its problems, without having to realize this negative truth. It is not merely that we have to confront many diverse notions of what constitutes the Church, many organizations bearing the one name, a multiplicity of traditions each claiming Church authenticity and authority—although this is true and has been noted to the point of triteness. No, it is not so much the diversity of forms in which the Church appears as the indubitable mystery manifest in them all that must give us pause. To speak of the Church at all in these days of the ecumenical encounter is inevitably to become aware of more than one level of meaning, perhaps even more than one realm of being, and to be asked to move back and forth between these realms or levels.

What is suggested here, it goes almost without saying, is the ancient distinction between the visible and the invisible Church. Despite the fact that this distinction has had different meanings to different groupings within the history of Christendom, what is noteworthy is that the distinction should have had to be made at all. Like all distinctions, this one is set up in the history of Christian thought for the purpose of marking a fundamental unity as well as an obvious diversity within the Church. Things may be said to differ in some respects only because they are alike in others. Especially when we are dealing with human matters it is important that distinctions should be kept fluid and under constant review. They tend to harden all too quickly into dualisms which are unreal and unfruitful for reflection, or they soften and merge into some fancied over-all unity, in which questions are answered before they have even been asked. There is very little rational hope in either process when pushed to the extreme.

When we think of the Church as being both visible and invisible we are suggesting, as we must, that neither term can properly exhaust the full meaning of the Church and that both together are needed to convey that meaning. This distinction has its value for theology in safeguarding the essentially mysterious character of the Church of Christ in speech and thought. The point it makes is that whatever may be said about the Church always leaves more to be said. There is more to this complex fact than meets the casual observer's eye; it does not all exist on its surface. Indeed, the use of this historic distinction chiefly means that the reality and the mystery of the Church are one and the same.

Neither side of this distinction, taken by itself, can bear the full weight of theological understanding. We cannot rest comfortably within the reassertion of the Church's invisible reality. The ecumenical movement, in its well-publicized initial victories, has been propelling some Christians much too rapidly toward a premature high-churchly stance. Possibly those of us who have been allowed a large amount of ecumenical exposure have fallen in love at first sight with types of belief about the Church which we do not yet, even tolerably, comprehend. At all events we seem to be willing to make affirmations about the catholicity or the holiness of the Church, for example, which nothing in our own immediate traditions can back up or justify. We may even catch ourselves saying things we do not honestly intend to say, in the glow of our new-found ecumenical enthusiasm. Hence we eagerly adopt as articles of faith concerning the Church convictions originating in other quarters; purely by virtue of their strangeness and in direct proportion to our own unsated ecumenical desires, we find these articles appealing. Belief in the "real presence" will be mentioned later on in this connection; other instances come quickly to mind as well.

One consequence of this overeager hospitality is that our words regarding the Church take on a tone, an unction, which our deeds of practical churchmanship cannot match. Thus the gap between our ecumenical profession and our organizational involvement, already quite apparent, is further widened. After a while we may lapse into confusing what we say with how we act, to our own detriment and that of those outside our fold. Despite our evident eagerness to talk and write as though they were identical or interchangeable, the *Una Sancta* and the church around the corner are as far apart as ever, maybe even further than before.

But neither can we be content with thinking of the Church as merely an empirical cluster of visible social entities. The "low" view that the Church is no more and no less than a voluntary association of believers comes to grief as soon as one begins to ask, "Believers in what or in whom?" This was made entirely clear more than a half century ago by the British Congregationalist P. T. Forsyth. He pointed out then the sacramental and Christological dimensions of the local congregation in a way suggestive of the Anglican thinker who preceded him, F. D. Maurice. Lest this be considered a matter of purely historical bearing it should be remarked that no stress upon the visibility of the Church has been able to do without a complementary insistence upon its invisibility, whether one has in mind social gospelers, Quakers, or the radical left wing of the Reformation.

At the present time, sociologists have been taking a long, hard look at our religious institutions. To our discomfiture they have been spelling out in unmistakable terms the ease with which these institutions adapt themselves to the dominant patterns and forces operating in our kind of world.

Rather generally, they report servility to cultural inertia and timidity toward cultural change among the actual churches. No one knows better than the active, loyal churchman himself just how true these findings are. Are we not devoted, day in, day out, to doing exactly what our own gospel tells us we ought not to be doing? Why be astonished if the social scientists see us as primarily good "organization men"? Publicizing the psychological if not material advantages of church membership, billboarding our righteousness, promoting an ever more expanding and successful religious enterprise—all this is precisely the sort of behavior against which the gospel throws a sharp question mark.

Why should this sociological critique become a reason for underscoring what may be called the hyphenated nature of the Church? Simply because we who operate mainly at the level of visibility cannot accept this judgment without being aware of the principles on which it is based. Criticism always presupposes criteria, and these may be all the more pertinent by virtue of the fact that they are largely hidden or implicit. Those who analyze and criticize the churches today do not simply parrot the going assumptions of, say, American culture. They are bearing curious, perhaps backhanded tribute to a view of the Church which they learned first from Christianity. This is the view that the Church, despite its failures and equivocations, ought to be about its Father's business like its Lord, that the actual Church should disclose more faithfully its divine intention and direction. But this is only another way of saying that the visible Church is really and mysteriously the bodying-forth, in our particular time and space, of the invisible Church.

Not many years ago it was my privilege to go by air from Copenhagen to Los Angeles on the polar route. After leaving Greenland there is a long stretch in the Atlantic waste that seems nearly filled with ice floes and icebergs. As I looked down upon those floating masses of ice, beyond the tip which was above the water, through the water, toward the base of the great moving object, I could grasp something of the totality which is an iceberg. What one hopes for in today's discussion of the Church, whether critical or enthusiastic, is a sharper and surer sense of its wholeness as a visible-invisible reality.

How may we claim to understand the Church, much less take part in its ongoing life, without some such intuition of its mysterious reality? It must be confessed that this sense is sadly lacking at the present time. Much too simply, the Church is lauded as a good thing by the devotees, or scored as a bad thing by the analyzers. To the discomfiture of both, may it not be made clear that each view is necessary and requires the other? Only so can something like the truth about the Church and the churches be discovered.

There have been at least three efforts in the history of Christian thought which commend themselves to theological attention today in grappling with the real mystery of the Church. One was that of St. Augustine, set forth most completely in his great and immeasurably influential work the *City of God.* The Church, he maintained, is placed between the earthly city and the heavenly city, embracing both yet belonging entirely to neither. However sharply St. Augustine might pose the antithesis between the two cities and the two loves on which they were founded, he insisted that the Church participates in both orders by its very nature as the community of God set down within the world of men. It is the peculiar necessity of the Church, out of which Christians must make a virtue, that it should look in two directions at once: toward the constellations of self-interest and group-interest that define the world, and also toward the intrusions of grace, of truth, and of love which disclose God's wisdom and power.

In one sense, according to this Augustinian perspective, the Church may be said to be trapped between these two orders. Love of God and love of man, however closely linked in

Christian theory, often appear to create acute tensions for our practical obedience. Only in Christ are they resolved. But since to be a Christian is to belong to Christ, this entrapment of the Church is also its opportunity and the ground of its vocation to be in and not of the world. For St. Augustine, as I have written elsewhere, "the Church . . . is only the crucial instance of that mysterious and constant interaction between God and man which is the substance of which everything historical is made."[1] Like man himself the Church is torn between conflicting loyalties, two orderings of life, one based, in E. R. Hardy's words, on the self-denying love of God, the other on the God-denying love of self. Yet what makes such conflict possible and such tension inevitable is the fact that the Church is required to live in both cities at once. Within it, therefore, the grain and the weeds must be permitted to grow together until the harvest, since God alone ultimately knows who are his and who are not.

The Augustinian vision has arresting pertinence for contemporary thought, because it preserves a needed balance and prevents escape into oversimple statements or solutions. Not only does this vision call in question easy generalizations about the oneness or the holiness of the Church as it stands in the world; it also, just as clearly, encourages hope on the part of those churches which are bogged down in the world, for it insists upon regarding the visible institution as an outpost of the invisible Kingdom which claims its primary allegiance.

Two historical echoes of this Augustinian vision deserve to be mentioned briefly in order to round out this conception. Those of us whose thinking about the Church is strongly influenced by the Protestant Reformation will be interested to learn that the traditional distinction between the visible and the invisible Church is central in the thought of Luther and Calvin. They based it, as might be expected, upon the doc-

[1] *Selected Writings of Saint Augustine* (Cleveland: Meridian Books, 1962), Introduction, p. 21.

trine of justification by faith. Only God knows those who truly live by faith; no ecclesiastical tests or measurements can presume to detect or decide this. In Reformation thought, in fact, the term "Body of Christ" means not the visible organization, but the Church unseen to human eyes and known alone to God. Calvin, of course, pushed this further than did Luther in his restatement of the doctrine of predestination, which is essentially a means of safeguarding God's sovereignty over his Church.

In recent years Paul Tillich has extended the Reformation idea by developing his theme of the "latent Church." As the Reformers tended to think of the invisible Church as somehow included within the visible, Tillich seeks to make plain that the invisible Church is wider than the visible. He wishes to take with utter seriousness our Lord's reminder, "Many sheep I have who are not of this fold." In this he is entirely true to St. Augustine who maintained that since the Church is both divinely intended and humanly conditioned we should not be surprised if "some things are done outside in the name of Christ not against the Church, and some things are done inside on the devil's part which are against the Church."[2] Thus no church is really Church which does not look beyond its visible frontiers in the direction of a Kingdom not of this world, and which does not recognize that nothing is out of bounds or off limits for God, who works silently and in secret to close the gap between the visible and invisible as he moves to accomplish his world-redeeming purpose.

2

Such is the context within which the relationship between the Church and Christ needs to be explored. We shall later see when discussing the corporate nature of Christian worship that we have to do with something as perplexing as it is pro-

[2] *On Baptism,* Book IV, chap. 10.

found. Hence the New Testament writers found it necessary to employ a multiplicity of images for this relationship, such as head and body, vine and branches, bridegroom and bride, and many others. These are not diverse illustrations of a common truth, nor do they all amount to saying the same thing theologically. Yet, as Paul Minear and others have shown, these images do reinforce and rectify each other; while they come very far from exhausting the subject they are indispensable for Christian reflection upon it. They accentuate the mysterious reality of the Church even as they suceed in penetrating it.

Here, however, we shall take another direction, not because the biblical images are unimportant, but because their very suggestiveness impels a frankly theological consideration. Assuredly the Church must be interpreted in terms of Jesus Christ or we would not be thinking seriously about the Church. But how shall this be done, with or without the help of scriptural metaphors and traditional symbols? If the Church is really a mystery, or mysteriously real, and if its nature is determined in relation to Christ, then it should be possible at least to locate or identify wherein the real mystery lies, even though it remains elusively itself.

In past ages theologians have pondered over this matter. It has seemed to them that the nature of the Church could be illuminated by the doctrine of the Word made flesh. There thus arose the view that the Church is actually the continuation of the Incarnation. In asking whether this view may be honestly reaffirmed today we are not merely reviving an ancient debate but entering into an acutely contemporary one. Within the ecumenical spectrum there are many churches, notably those belonging to the Catholic traditions, for whom it is necessary to believe that the Church in its very existence continues and extends the life of God incarnate in the Christ. What is emphasized in this view is nothing less than the divinity of the Church, if this rather startling phrase may be used here. The Son of God did not vanish from history at his resurrection and ascension; he gave life to the Church so that it might prolong and fulfill the divine intention which had become incarnate in himself. In word and sacrament, witness and mission, Christ is virtually extending himself in the Church, so that it becomes quite difficult for the Catholic tradition finally to distinguish the Church from Christ at all.

On this side of the current debate one finds not only representatives of such churches as the Anglican, Orthodox, and Roman Catholic, but also, surprisingly perhaps, those of "free" churches like the Congregational. On the other side stand Baptists and Disciples, who do not subscribe to the view that the Church is the extension of the Incarnation except in an extremely figurative sense. In this group also belong the Presbyterians, who would disallow the belief completely, and the Methodists, for whom the sanctifying power of the Holy Spirit takes the place of continued Incarnation in the Catholic sense.

There is then a fairly marked divergence of views among the churches on this article of belief, and their exposure to each other in the ecumenical encounter is tending to force the issue. It would seem that in most pronouncements coming from ecumenical bodies the Catholic position is predominant, either implicitly or explicitly. What should be our own conclusion?

Let us take a closer look at the Catholic view, which holds to the divinity of the Church. The claim is not that the Church is identical with God, but that God has bestowed something of his own nature upon the Church. It has been given the "keys of the Kingdom," Christ's authority to bind and loose, to save and judge the world. Its marks of holiness, unity, apostolicity, and catholicity bear testimony to that. One could almost say that, according to this view, without us in the Church Christ himself cannot be made perfect. What happens to the once-for-allness of the Incarnation if it is still going on? Is the Word made flesh in Christ alone, or perpetually remade flesh within the Church? Are we to say that in the world of here-and-now, the Church is all the Christ there is?

Questions like these are forced upon us by the Catholic view that the Church continues the Incarnation. To some extent, to be sure, that view is borne out by the New Testament. When Jesus on the cross said, "It is finished," he could not have meant that his work of salvation was over and done with, for in a true sense it had only begun. On the cross the heart of the matter had been laid bare, to be sure; the grip of guilty, deathly evil had been broken by the suffering, saving love of God himself toward men. The eyes of faith perceive the death of Christ through the lens of the resurrection, as being victory over death. Precisely by becoming obedient to death, Christ set at naught its final power over men. But this does not mean that mankind is henceforth free from the necessity of dying, or that there are no battles with sin and guilt still to be won. Although the work of Christ was conclusive, as Nels Ferré says, it was not concluded. The Church must still engage in long, bitter conflict with those dark powers which Christ in his own person challenged and overcame, knowing in God's good time he will give us the Kingdom. As it takes up the struggle the Church is charged to speak and act for Christ in order that his triumph may be ours also.

But is it necessary, in Christian faith, to guarantee the ultimate victory of God at the end of history by positing the divinity of the Church in the interim between Christ's first and second coming? That is the real question. Let us agree that the Church is truly intended and instituted by its Lord to be the very means of God's grace and the sure hope of his glory. Let us agree further that in Christ God did not merely pay the earth a temporary visit but changed the dynamics of history, shifted the balance of power, released the permanent possibility of new being, restored the goodness of original creation, so that the world is forever different from what it was before his taking of our flesh upon himself. Once more, let us agree that Christ has given his Spirit to the mysterious reality, set down in history, which is called the Church, so that it truly carries and conveys the thrust of God's amazing love in and for the world. But whether all this adds up to the conviction that the Church is the extension of the Incarnation is the question at issue.

The question may be put in still another way. Can the Church participate in Christ's servanthood without also sharing in his Lordship? Does the familiar theological distinction between the nature and the work of Christ have any real validity in spelling out his relationship with his Church, or not? There is, of course, a sure insight behind the hesitation to separate too sharply the person of Christ from his work. What Christ does and who he is belong together in our faith and therefore also in our thought. Christmas and the cross are indissolubly linked at the heart of the Christian gospel. Each sheds necessary and important light upon the other.

Yet some working distinction between Christ's person and his mission does need to be made. Incarnation is not itself atonement, although it is the ground and the occasion for atonement. And atonement is not itself incarnation, even if it is the consequence and purpose of incarnation. These doctrinal terms should be used with some fidelity to the concrete complexity and historicity of what is called the total Christ-event. They do not mean the same thing even though they may come to the same thing in the end.

When we are considering the relationship between the Church and Christ, this distinction becomes indispensable. The Church, like any other human institution, has a certain tendency to magnify and even to glorify itself inordinately. Those outside the institution are generally more conscious of this tendency than those within. The only inner safeguard against it is that provided by the gospel in its warning that we must not think more highly of ourselves than we ought to think. It is no part of the gospel, or of faith based upon it, that the Church is consubstantial with its Lord or that its status as well as its originating purpose is divine. In Karl Barth's telling phrase, between the Church and Christ there is no reversible, interchangeable relationship, as certainly the relation between master and servant is not reversible.[3] We must not be hurried into any position which would regard the Church as indistinguishable from Christ himself.

The best way of avoiding such an untenable position is to utilize the distinction between the person and the work of Christ in setting forth our understanding of the Church. There is real merit at this point in the current slogan that the Church's nature is its mission. If the very being of the Church is that discovered in its acting, that is, in what it is sent into the world to do for God, then it is scarcely right to identify the Church completely with him who sends it forth on his errand, commissions it, and puts it under orders. Either the Church is subordinate to God in Christ or it is simply not the Church. It is known by what it does, and what it has to do is given by its Lord. This "sentness" of the Church, when taken with real seriousness, forbids us the presumption of thinking that the Church may ever be confused with him who does the sending. There is hardly any distinction more sharp and decisive, at least on the level of human will and choice, than that between command and obedience.

Therefore it is humbler and wiser to declare that the Church is the continuation of the atoning work of Christ than to hold that it is the extension of the Incarnation. What is continued in the Church is Christ's own ministry of reconciling and renewing love for all the world. This is its charter of salvation. It is far more defensible, theologically and morally, to maintain this than to press what Reinhold Niebuhr calls "the deification of the Church." It is the servanthood of Christ continued in the Church which is voiced in

[3] *The Doctrine of the* Word *of God,* in *Church Dogmatics* I/2 (New York: Charles Scribner's Sons, 1956), p. 113.

the preaching of the word and lifted up in the celebration of the sacrament. We are not called in the Church to regard equality with God as something to be grasped; we are called to do God's work through the power of his Spirit set free in the world by Christ. If this may be thought of as the continuation of the Incarnation of the Son of God, it is only in a mediated and refracted sense. To be sure, the Church both visible and invisible exists by reason of the Incarnation and in continuous faith-relationship to it, but the Church is not itself the Incarnation extended or prolonged in history.

Is it possible, within the perspective thus afforded by distinguishing between the work and person of Christ, to do full justice to the historic stress upon the invisible, divine dimension of the Church? Let us, in the remainder of this chapter, take up the task of making good an affirmative answer to this question.

3

Consider, in the first place, the truth which biblical theologians have lately been emphasizing—that the Church is a part of the gospel itself. The New Testament proclamation concerning what God has done for us in Christ not only implies the Church but presupposes it as well. That proclamation is made by the new-found community gathered in the name of Jesus, acknowledging him as Lord, awaiting his return, and finding in his will and work the very motivation of their own. Theologically, the gospel takes precedence over the Church; but chronologically, in point of fact, the Church gives shape and substance to the proclamation of the gospel.

Scholars are in disagreement as to what Jesus' own intention was regarding the Church. Perhaps a thoroughly factual answer will never be reached. Some hold that he was the Church's founder, that it represents not only his but God's intention and must therefore claim divine authority and sanction. Other scholars maintain, on the contrary, that Jesus neither instituted nor foresaw the Church, as the very idea of the Church is foreign to his entire teaching and example. Yet there is a growing body of scholarship which takes a position somewhere between these contradictory extremes. Although this group of scholars denies that the Church as it developed was that which was planned by the Lord, the point is nevertheless made that Jesus did call into being a fellowship which thereafter did become the Church as we know it. Surely it was not merely accidental or ironical that this should have taken place as it did, since the Lord himself had constituted the "little flock" to whom he meant to "give the Kingdom." This moderate position appears completely tenable in light of such biblical evidence as we possess.

Jesus' own calling of the disciples and sending them forth "as sheep among wolves" provides at least a significant clue. Like the disciples, the Church lives by a double process of being gathered and then scattered, of *koinonia* and *diakonia*, each centered in its Lord. Whether or not a full-fledged sacramental institution may have been in Jesus' mind, a community as the nucleus of faith most certainly was, unless we are to dismiss a major part of the New Testament writings as irrelevant in answering this question. The good news he brought to men, for all its inwardness, dealt not with private beliefs or solitary behavior but with neighborly conduct and and brotherly concern. The Kingdom, which was the burden of so much of Jesus' teaching, is an obviously social if also heavenly reality, embracing and yet cutting across the natural groupings of mankind. Considerations like these lead us rather definitely to the conclusion that Jesus intended and indeed instituted a new form of human community anchored in God's radically redemptive love revealed in his own life and work. To deny outright that this is so could only mean that one had not really heard the gospel as it stands forth in the pages of the Bible.

This is what is meant, and all that is meant, in declaring that the Church is a part of the gospel. Scholars have done much to sort out the various layers of tradition both oral and written which are embodied in our New Testament, so that it can be said that as a matter of historical sequence the gospel is tradition even before it becomes Scripture. What is set down in the gospel is that a new Israel, fulfilling but not destroying the old, a wholly new sort of bond among men, is God's will for the world revealed in Christ. And this new ordering of life about the crucified and risen Lord is not alone announced but actually initiated and carried forward into the new age that has already begun.

Yet reflect upon what this inauguration of the new community does and does not involve. Clearly, it affords little if any excuse for ecclesiastical self-justification. The fact that the Church is part of the gospel encourages neither arrogance nor complacency regarding any particular organization, practice, or belief. A recent conversation on the meaning of baptism, involving representatives from six different denominations, resulted in the agreement that no sure warrant could be found in Scripture for one preferred mode of baptism as over against another, nor for the exclusion of either infant or adult baptism as without biblical support. Surprisingly perhaps, the members of this consultation discovered that they had hit upon a liberating, not a threatening, word. They felt relieved of the embarrassment of having to repeat old shibboleths and special pleadings, out of mistaken loyalty to some fragment of the gospel in preference to the whole. That experience is a fair sample of many others taking place within the present ecumenical context. Greatly helped by biblical scholarship, which sees the Church as part of the gospel itself, we can now abandon partisan bibliolatry, doctrinaire liturgics, and all other atavistic efforts to justify each and every churchly status quo in terms of sanctions presumed to come from the gospel. The situation is certainly healthy, not to say refreshing.

If we really believe that the Church is the will of God as disclosed in the gospel, however, there is a further step to be taken. For it follows "as the night the day" that if we must not willfully seek to harness Church to gospel, then we should more willingly let the gospel speak and work through the Church. Here once again the essential mystery of the Church appears. As a social structure it houses itself, maintains its identity, provides for its continuity and increase, all for the sake of the gospel which it professes and shares with the world. Living as the community or "peculiar people" of faith in God's deed in Christ, the Church learns over and over again that it cannot live only for itself. It is in going out from itself, indeed, that the Church discovers and rediscovers the very meaning of its own existence. Is the Church less itself when it endeavors to penetrate and permeate the world with the very message and mission of its Lord? No, it is more itself, more what God intends and commands it to be.

Assuredly the best and clearest way to understand this twofold and mysterious character of the Church is with the help of the central thrust of the gospel. How may we avoid believing that the Church is actually most itself when it is least itself—least concerned with its own righteousness before God, least anxious about its own tomorrow, least given to excusing its faults and parading its virtues? Does not the principle of mastery through servanthood, of exaltation through humility, apply *a fortiori* to the being of the Church? If it does, the fact must be accepted and, as the current jargon has it, "implemented" that the Church is able to live its own life only as it lives for others, for the world. By possessing its soul in patience and seeking to maintain its purity and integrity as the household of God, the Church is doing a good thing; but by going out from itself bearing the food and drink of the gospel, the Church is doing a better thing. And the fact that it can do the latter only if it has done the former, that it can be sent abroad only if it is first there and available for God's errands, ought not to obscure our sense of what the true priorities must be.

George Macleod has expressed this so tellingly that his words deserve to be recalled here:

> I simply argue that the Cross be raised again at the center of the market place as well as on the steeple of the church. I am recovering the claim that Jesus was not crucified in a cathedral between two candles, but on a cross between two thieves; on the town garbage heap; at a crossroad so cosmopolitan that they had to write his title in Hebrew and in Latin and in Greek; . . . at the kind of place where cynics talk smut, and thieves curse, and soldiers gamble. Because that is where he died. And that is what he died about. And that is where churchmen should be and what churchmen should be about.[4]

At this point the theologically alert reader may have a question to ask. As right and moving as it is, does not this whole appeal to the Church to take upon itself the "dying form" of its Lord reopen the matter of a prolonged or extended Incarnation? Are we not then caught defending the divinity of the Church after all?

I still do not believe that this is either necessary or imperative. There is no fateful logic driving us to the position that since the Church shares in Christ's work it must share his nature *en morphe theou.* To repeat what was said earlier, Church and Christ are clearly not interchangeable terms. Christ does give, through faith, the Church his work to do, and it *is* his work; but the difference and the distance between the servant and the servant Lord are not so easily annulled as we may think or wish. That the form of the servant is common to both is due not primarily to the Church's own faithfulness, standing steadfast for centuries and centuries, but to Christ's Lordship which makes such steadfastness possible. Our servanthood within the Church is actually a double or compounded one; it is not Christ who belongs to the Church, but the Church which belongs to Christ.

Yes, the Church is part of the gospel, but the gospel is not

[4] *Only One Way Left* (The Iona Community, n.d.), p. 38.

part of the Church. How could it be, when it is the very reason for the Church's own existence in the world? The gospel is given to the Church to proclaim, not to possess. Moreover, the Church always remains under the judgment of the gospel; its "authority" is never to be separated either in thought or in deed from its obedient fidelity to the gospel. There can be no question as to what comes first in truth and right. It is the gospel which precedes and determines the Church, even if it is through the Church that mankind learns what the gospel is.

4

There is a further consideration looking toward a reawakened conviction that the Church is specially included in God's plan for bringing new, abundant life to all mankind, as this plan is disclosed in Christ. It has to do with a better understanding of St. Paul's great image of the Church as the Body of Christ, an image which despite much contemporary exposition is still very far from being grasped clearly.

Scholars disagree, and quite possibly always will, on whether this Pauline figure constitutes a metaphor of the Church or a definition capable of bearing total theological weight. They seem to be agreed, however, that it is no mere simile, at least in the mind of Paul himself. But frequently in current theological discussion we have been presented with what appears to be a forced option and asked to choose, on the basis of our interpretation of this image, between contradictory conceptions of the Church. If it is metaphorical only, then we are urged to opt for a view of the Church that is both "low" and "free." But if it actually has the force of a definition, then, we are told, we become Catholics in spite of ourselves. The essential holiness, apostolicity, and unity of the Church are thereby supposed to be authenticated.

In the light of St. Paul's own use of this compelling image I do not see how the option can be regarded as forced. In fact, the more seriously we take it the more we shall find it saying not one but several things. Ostensibly and redundantly, it means incorporation; this is the meaning upon which some writers have fixed so enthusiastically of late, without pausing to reflect upon the mysterious character of the body as "presence." But there are other meanings too, none of which should be dismissed from Christian memory or motivation. One is that of mutuality. To be in the body of Christ is to have what Dietrich Bonhoeffer called "life together"—e.g., to draw my own life from the lives of others and to give it back again, in such a way that the good of each becomes the good of all, as H. N. Wieman likes to put it. When St. Paul writes, "Now you are the body of Christ, and individually members of it," he is not referring to any monolithic or mechanical reality. Quite the opposite; he means that to be members of the Body is to be members of one another. Nothing could be plainer, and it is important for our understanding of life in the Church. Mutuality involves each one of us in the rest of mankind; that is the obvious and moral meaning of the Pauline image. For the Christian it signifies that membership is inseparable from discipleship, that we have life in common because of our common Lord, and by means of grace through faith.

Again, the cherished figure of St. Paul embraces the meaning of organic growth. In its light the Church is seen to have a life of its own, holding within itself its potency for good or evil, and yet never wholly identical with its past or future. So in the parables of Jesus, the Kingdom of which the Church is the harbinger is spoken of as a growing thing requiring time for its realization and yet bursting the bonds of time. To be in the Body of Christ, therefore, is to be caught up in processes that develop and augment and invoke the coming Kingdom. The living, growing wholeness of the Church is due to its God-given relationship with him whom St. Paul, following out his image, called the head or source of mind and will.

Let us shape the thought embedded in this image still further. As the Body of Christ the Church is not transparent but opaque to God. It is no ideal, purely "spiritual" community capable of being grasped by bloodless categories. Neither can it be supposed to subsist above, or to be immune to, the web of social and historic actualities in which it all too plainly is enmeshed. A body has location, density, configuration; so does the Church. It cannot be everywhere at once or open equally to all possible influences; neither can the Church. How seldom is this recognized in present-day church architecture! But put Le Corbusier's pilgrim chapel at Ronchamp, France, hugging its hill with its mushroomlike roof, beside the "chicken-coop contemporary" of a church building in a nondescript American suburb, and the point will be well made. No view of the Church can presume to be Christian which fails to comprehend its bodily, even earthly character. Lacking such comprehension it is easy to fall into the same kind of heresy, called Docetism, which refused to believe in our Lord's real and individual humanity. The image of the Church as the Body of Christ will always be important because it makes a standing protest against any effort to glorify the Church by making it seem even purer or nobler than its Lord.

These meanings are bound up closely in the visible word which is the sacrament called the Eucharist, or The Lord's Supper. Although it is often considered to be the celebration of the Incarnation, it is more fittingly regarded as the dramatic re-presenting of the Atonement. What it signifies most centrally is that we are incorporated into the work of Christ in an act "between memory and hope." In it we show forth the Lord's death until he comes. The symbols used are those of the body—flesh broken, blood shed for the saving of many by the death of one. The words of institution give us a summary, terse yet rich, of the whole plan of God's redeeming work in Christ. The action of the congregation is of all events the most common, but it is informed with quite uncommon significance—eating and drinking "to eternal life." Thus it is shown forth that the Church participates in the momentum of redemption through Jesus Christ our Lord.

Is it a question of "real presence"? Yes, but we should understand that such presence does not attach in the first instance to the elements employed; it, rather, is linked to the corporate, sacramental action itself. We may almost say that in the Eucharist the Church continually recreates the crisis and the opportunity for faith in Christ; certainly they are made present again. And it is neither an exclusively Protestant nor an exclusively Roman Catholic but a fully Christian principle that in the sacrament God does not move to save man by denying the physical creation but by using and blessing it, as exemplified in these fruits of human toil and sustenance and enjoyment. "Presence" here means sacrifice, "making holy" by the energies of grace.

And how is this to be done? Only by taking Christ's work to ourselves as nourishment for our daily pilgrimage and warfare. In Pascal's words, "I must add my wounds to his, and join myself to him; and he will save me in saving himself." Or as St. Paul expressed the same imperative, we must "fill up what is lacking in the sufferings of Christ." What might seem blasphemy when applied to the person of Christ is no more than faithful obedience when linked to his work. True, liturgical action is not to be confused with lifelong servanthood, and yet it may powerfully illumine and inspire such devoted service in a way that is altogether indispensable to our behavior and relationships "here below."

Is it not entirely clear that this refusal to equate the Church with Christ by no means entails a "low" view of the Church? On the contrary, it places the Church in the highest possible light. No more should be expected or demanded than that the Christian be allowed to take part in the burden-bearing, joy-sharing task of human reconciliation and restoration itself. Our claim is only that Christ works through us, lives in us, in order that we may live and work for him. Call this claim "mystical" if you like; buttress it as you will by theories of transubstantiation or sanctification; but do not hopelessly confuse the servant with his Lord.

St. Paul, in calling the Church the Body of Christ, gave us an image that suggests the mystery of intimate dependence upon Christ which is utterly necessary to the Church's ongoing life, while also holding fast to the complementary mystery of sovereign headship on the part of Christ. Lest we be tempted to think more highly of ourselves than we ought to think, we are thereby reminded that the Church is its Lord's body and no more. But lest we be prone to despair in the face of so much that is evil or destructive in ourselves and the world, we are assured that our Lord is related to us as closely, as integrally, as a human self is linked to its own body.

The depths of meaning in this mystery will never be completely sounded. That is because the better we understand it the greater the mystery becomes. How can we finally comprehend that by which we ourselves are comprehended? Yet real beginnings can be made. The Church may resolve to become in fact what it already is in principle, the Body of Christ. Unless the visible Church can remain corporeal to its invisible Lord, it will be no more than a corpse.

In order to make more fully clear the bearing of St. Paul's great image upon our common faith and life, we shall require the help of the doctrine of the Holy Spirit. Here, as so often in theology, it is this doctrine which is able to keep our thought in proper balance and perspective. A true, though never total, understanding of the Christ-Church relationship must be in terms of spirit as well as body. There can be no confidence that the Church extends throughout history the thrust of God's loving deed in Christ without faith that this becomes possible by the continual empowering of his Spirit. In the next chapter we shall hope to give convincing substance to this faith.

CHAPTER III

Christ and the Spirit

It is not too much to say that of all the themes which are treated in Christian theology, the Holy Spirit is at once the most obscure and the most urgent. Although worn smooth by centuries of pious repetition, the word "spirit" has ceased to engage our minds or to stir our hearts. Where it does not actually baffle us as used in church services, it simply leaves us cold, because it sets up no reverberations of meaning except the most conventional or lethargic. Indeed, it seems that we have been anesthetized against taking this word seriously and honestly as pointing toward any recognizable reality.

How, if at all, may "spirit" be rehabilitated as a meaningful word? Certainly not by setting it in opposition to "matter" or "body" in the usual fashion. This can only encourage the notion that spirit is *non*material, *dis*embodied, ghostly. Such an approach is all too plainly based on the general prejudice of our age that what cannot be seen or handled is less real than what can be. This *is* a prejudice and can be shown to be so, but it has been taken for granted so long by so many people that it appears almost self-evident, at least until a few of its consequences are thought through.

There are better ways of understanding what is meant by spirit. Common speech contains a number of clues. "Spirits of ammonia," the "spirit" of a meeting, the "spirit" of a man or an age—all these convey the essence or gist of something, its most concentrated and hence most real form. If, for example, I speak of the spirit of Abraham Lincoln I am not referring to his ghost, whatever that is, but to the very kind of man he was, his unique self. As we know, it is often only after one has died that his spirit becomes actually plain to us; during his lifetime he may be so harnessed in relationships and so hindered by circumstances that it is hard to see him as the person he is. Mark Twain, you may remember, put this in a rather bitter way. He remarked that most of us are never really ourselves until we are dead. And he added that perhaps we ought to start dead so that we could begin being ourselves sooner. Several years ago a book by a well-known television comic was published just before Easter. Its title was *Is There Life after Birth?* That is a question about spirit.

Spirit, then, should not be taken to mean ghostliness, not aftermath, not distant, shadowy, second-rate reality. In the Christian context, at least, it signifies the heart of a matter, the thing itself, the quality of something real which gives to it its peculiar and original sort of reality. Whenever the Bible says "spirit" it says active energy, genuine influence, "life." This is the point at which our Christian thinking on the subject must begin.

1

God is a Spirit, the Scriptures repeat many times. He cannot be seen but he can be felt, known, and responded to in personal encounter. He is "nearer to us than breathing, and closer than hands or feet." He is "with us," which suggests not existing alongside but intimate involvement, perhaps even indwelling. The conception of God as Spirit has a great many modulations in the Bible. Scholars have shown that it has primitive roots in the words for "wind" and "breath," which signify God's unseen influence and active energy. So, like a wind, the Spirit of God broods over the face of the waters at the world's creation. He may also express himself in righteous wrath: "With the breath of his mouth he will slay the wicked." But the Spirit may be unitive and gathering as well as destroying and scattering, as at Pentecost when "a mighty rushing wind" fashions together a new people and imparts the gift of new insight sweeping away old barriers of culture and language.

But we are not primitives, or at least we like to think that we are not; and what does this notion of God as Spirit, admittedly ancestral, have to do with us? Granted that we can speak intelligently of the spirit of a man, meaning his inmost reality, but what do crude metaphors of a bygone day have to tell us about God? Suppose that the biblical images and terms of reference are not to be taken literally, for they are designed precisely to evoke the sense of mystery and not to remove it; the question then becomes whether biblical words can still be taken seriously. Or are we Christians, like the French monk in the market place, "simply trying to keep alive the rumor that there is a God"?

There might be worse occupations for Christians than that, but surely we must at least attempt something better. Can we not in any case know what we are saying when we say that God is Spirit? If we do, it will not be because we have arrived at a general definition of "spirit" into which the definition of God may be conveniently fitted; instead it will be because we "know in whom we have believed" as offering us a definitive disclosure of God's Spirit. In other words, Christ discloses or reveals the way God deals with us and acts upon us. If we did not believe this we should be quite unable to "test the spirits," to distinguish a true from a lying inspiration; and what is more, we would not have any particular, that is, personally compelling, reason for entertaining belief in either spirit or God.

This brings us to the first proposition to be laid down in

this chapter: The Spirit of God is disclosed in Christ. That may seem safe enough within the covers of a book on Christian theology, but actually it is a most far-ranging and deeply fertile truth, as will become evident presently. For Christ's revealing of the Spirit of God, that is, of the very Godhood of God, is significant in at least two basic senses: it is permanent and it is universal. Each of these deserves the clearest, most careful thought.

The permanence of the disclosure of God's Spirit in Jesus Christ needs to be viewed in biblical perspective. It stands in marked contrast to the prophetic visitations reported in the Old Testament, although these are clearly a preparation for it. The prophetic visitations of the Spirit were sporadic, irregular, and unpredictable. An Ezekiel, for example, might be "caught up in the Spirit" for a long moment of ecstatic vision, but there is always the supposition that he might be let down again; indeed, we have in the prophetic work of Jeremiah a record of his bitter sense of being abandoned by the very God who had commissioned him. Although God may put words in the prophet's mouth, the prophet remains no more than God's mouthpiece, his instrument of judgment or of healing, as the case may be. Also, a prophet's authority is derived from God and may be withdrawn, even if the words "Thus saith the Lord" suggest that human and divine speaking have temporarily become identical in prophecy.

There are, to be sure, genuine premonitions in the Old Testament of a permanent and settled disclosure of God's Spirit operating within a given individual or group. In Second Isaiah we are told that the Spirit will descend upon and *remain with* the messianic servant-figure. As is well known, it is an open question whether and to what extent the messianic servant is to be identified with the remnant-group in Israel or with a future personal bearer of the newly announced reign of God. But in any case we do not have, except eschatologically in the form of a promise to be realized later, the assurance that God's Spirit takes up permanent residence in any single human being.

It is very different in the New Testament. The baptism of Jesus at the hands of John is the occasion for the descent of the Spirit upon him, in the form of a dove, the ancient symbol of God's covenanted promise to restore humanity. Despite the early Christian heresy of adoptionism—the view that at the moment of baptism, or at some other time, God "adopts" Christ into the status of Sonship—the language of the Gospels plainly indicates that the descent of the dove is meant as a visible revelation that Jesus is in truth the permanent bearer of God's Spirit. It is precisely in this sense that Jesus is seen to be "a prophet, and more than a prophet." He does not receive the active energy of God as a borrowed or conditional gift which might be taken away again; no, Jesus is forever he who bears and who carries forward the Spirit of God into man's total existence. He is, in short, the permanent disclosure of the Spirit, the "*habitation* of the most High."

Perhaps this is the right place to speak about the relationship between God's Spirit and the human spirit, in the biblical understanding. The term "spirit" is common to both man and God; that is abundantly clear. But human spirit is no mere extension or duplication of the divine; the reason such an assertion must not be made is that spirit in man is the source of his sin as well as his capacity to receive grace. Wickedness is no less spiritual than is righteousness; we have a very faint, attenuated echo of this when we refer to a "highly intelligent criminal." The point is that while human spirit bespeaks or connotes God as its origin and goal, it also evidences man's potential enmity to God, his *libido* or driving wish to be his own God. Today, one of the most common synonyms for "spirit" is "freedom"; and we well know how involuntary our volition is, how undecided our power of decision, how ambiguous our freedom.

As always, it is the question as to what being human means. To Christian faith this means "spirit"—that which is imparted to us by God's gracious outpouring of his own life in his Son. Nikolai Berdyaev has written that the revelation of God to man is the reciprocal revelation of man in God; and so, in Jesus Christ, it surely is. It is to God that we owe our full humanity, and it is through Christ that we know this to be so. And this is not a once-upon-a-time sort of statement, but actually a very present truth. Man, too, is a spirit, and this means that he becomes himself not by summoning up his own self-generating powers but by relationship to him who is the Maker, Lover, and Keeper of all life. This is expressed with great beauty by the Psalmist: "The spirit of man is the candle of the Lord." One should be wary of literalizing, and so vulgarizing, a metaphor like this, but at least it means that human spirit needs and awaits the touch of Holy Spirit to kindle it to life and so to realization of itself. What makes man fully, really human, so that, as Pascal wrote, his very wretchedness is a strange kind of greatness, is what comes to him from God.

Christ has given us not only a new definition of God but also a new definition of man, because in him the Spirit actively engages, searches out, and saves the human precisely by becoming enmanned. In him it is made permanently and indelibly plain that God is the God of men, our God.

The disclosure of God's Spirit in Christ is more than permanent; it is universal as well. If a scriptural text is needed as a basis for this assurance, it is of course the passage in Joel 2:28: "I will pour out my spirit on all flesh." These words are remembered and underscored at Pentecost, the birthday of the Church. They point to Spirit as the sign of God's unbelievable bounty, his overflowing generosity toward mankind as such. They express once again the truth that God's being *is* his acting, his "essence" is his outpouring. The prophetic vision promises a sharing of God's Spirit that is manwide and world-deep, prefiguring the "universalism" of the good news brought by Christ.

A defensive orthodoxy shudders when it hears the word

"universalism," and would like to label it a heresy, a perversion of the gospel. The reason is not far to seek: namely, the fear that God's self-giving love may be thought undiscriminating, that the faithful will be offered no special incentive or reward, and that God's righteous judgment visited upon sin is thereby abrogated or annulled. It is also felt that "universalism" denies the all too obvious fact that some men say No to God's Spirit even when it is poured out upon them and they ought to be held accountable or be punished for their sinful rejection. What becomes of hell if there are no lines drawn, no final warnings given—if, in short, God's loving Spirit is thought to be bestowed without either wrath or judgment?

Karl Barth's reply to his critics on this point still seems to me the best. "This much is certain," he writes, "that we have no theological right to set any sort of limits to the loving-kindness of God which has appeared in Jesus Christ. Our theological duty is to see and understand it as being still greater than we had seen before."[1] The disclosure of God's Spirit in Christ is for all people, is upon all flesh. To be sure, it may be rejected but it cannot be set at naught by men. If this appears to make hell a matter of doubt rather than an article of faith, so much the worse for hell! At all events, our "theological duty" is clear; we know where we must begin and where we have to end in thinking about God's self-disclosure in Christ. The doctrinal chips will have to fall wherever they may.

There are dangers to be guarded against, as in every theological statement, and it is important that we know what we are saying and are understood by Christians and non-Christians alike. The doctrine that Christ is the universal disclosure of God's Spirit should not be taken to mean some kind of religious syncretism. We are not saying that Christ is only a name for what might otherwise be described as God-in-general manifesting himself to man-in-general. The historical

[1] *The Humanity of God* (Richmond Va.: John Knox Press, 1960), p. 62.

and specific uniqueness of Christ is not so easily dispensable. Rather, we believe with W. A. Visser 'tHooft that "humanity by itself cannot realize its desire for true universality." Therefore we see in Christ the radical demand of God for man's explicit obedience, the "narrow way" by which all nations and peoples are to realize their new and true humanity.

Neither are we saying that when God pours out his Spirit upon all flesh he simply distributes himself gratis, gives himself away in equal parts so that every human being possesses as it were a little piece of God. That is not what either human spirit or Holy Spirit means. It is in Christ and through Christ that God's imparting of his Spirit takes place, because Christ is the *enmanment* of God. Men sort themselves out by the nature of their response to this deed-gift of God's universal love, but God retains his initiative and sovereignty in giving it. Whatever else God may be, he is not man's possession or prerogative. The mystery of godly love, whenever and wherever it appears, is that, like Moses' bush, it is burned but not consumed, for it grows in being spent.

The Incarnation did not happen to the man Jesus, but it happened in him. Its particularity, while not to be discounted, needs to be understood as being exactly its universality. That is what makes Christ unique, that in him "once *for all*" the way of our redemption was entered and opened. The whole world is a decisively different world because of what took place in Christ. No fact in it remains the same; no event is left untouched. That is because, in Christ, God has poured out his Spirit upon all flesh, curling the corners of the earth and shrinking the ends of time.

This brings us to the central matter of this chapter. Let me introduce it by mentioning a contrast which P. T. Forsyth was fond of drawing, that between Word and Spirit as referring to God's act in Christ. Forsyth liked to distinguish quite sharply the Word as God's self-definition from the Spirit as God's self-diffusion. He even applied this distinction to church polity, pointing out how some churches were founded theologically upon God's binding himself to us in Christ, and how others were grounded in his freely giving himself to us in Christ. If in his Word God tells us who he really is, in his Spirit he gives us "power to become."

We are quite accustomed to hearing it said that Christ is God's Word, and with good reason, but the relation between Christ and the Spirit has caused no little difficulty throughout the history of Christian thought. Indeed, it was divergence on this issue which resulted in the separation of Eastern from Western Christendom, focused in the debate over the *filioque* clause in the creed. Did the Holy Spirit "proceed" from the Father through the Son, or jointly from both Father and Son? Before this is dismissed as a dead issue or a mere semantic squabble, let us see what was actually at stake. The question had to do with whether Christ as Son of God was only the bearer or conveyor of God's Spirit or, on the other hand, its co-author and donor. And this, as a puzzled professor might say, is a "good question." It is so because there is real danger for both thought and faith in separating too distinctly, too confidently, the Word and the Spirit of God vouchsafed to us in Christ. We know that they do—and should—mean different things, but both things must be meant.

As a matter of fact the *filioque* controversy represents another stage in the continuing Trinitarian discussion which took shape in the early centuries of the Church. It is perhaps one of the ironies of history that the Trinity was intended to safeguard theologically the unity of God, but as it works out this doctrine seems rather to complicate and befuddle Christian thought by generating ever new problems. If a thinker leans just a bit too heavily upon the oneness of God, then Father, Son, and Spirit quickly tend to become phases which succeed each other in time. But if the threeness of God is held before the mind too rigidly, then Father, Son, and Spirit soon take on a kind of representational distinctness of their own, becoming almost parts of Deity as a whole. It is hard, but highly necessary, to avoid all this chronologizing and segmenting of the triune God, this vulgarizing of the doctrine of the Trinity.

However, these difficulties must be boldly and deftly faced. One good way to do this would appear to be through a more careful delineation of what Word and Spirit may be said to mean with respect to each other, remembering that these are at best but faith-metaphors for probing ancient, irreducible mysteries. Word and Spirit, to use Barth's phrase, are "God's ways of being God." They are with God at the beginning, "before" there is a world, which is why they figure in the biblical saga of creation. Yet they receive their right names and are truly known for what they are only at the Incarnation of God in Jesus Christ. Then it becomes clear what God has been saying all along, how and why he has been acting for our final good. The Word means God speaking, laying his ultimate claim on man, summoning man out of estrangement into conclusive fellowship; the Spirit means God acting, sharing his very life with us, empowering us from within to do the truth that has been addressed to us. Both Word and Spirit, taken together, are indispensable for Christian understanding of the person and work of Christ. And both refer, implicitly and explicitly, to the Christian fact that it is the Spirit of God who speaks universally in Christ, as his Word of grace and truth dwells universally among us, "spiritually" in Christ.

2

A further conviction which needs to be spelled out in this chapter has to do with what may be called the Spirit of Christ in the Church. If we should ask why Christians have a doctrine of the Holy Spirit at all, the answer must be that they wish to understand their experience of aliveness, of the Lord being alive, in the Church. It is no accident that in the creed the mention of belief in the Church falls under the heading of the third article on the Spirit—even though the order of arrival at such belief may seem to have been the other way around. The Church's experience of Christ is always outrunning its theological comprehension of this experience; the task of theology is therefore that of catching up with the "movering" of the Spirit in and through the Church.

As believers our relationship to Christ is carried forward through the power of his Spirit present and active in our midst. At least this seems the only way in which we can comprehend the possibility and actuality of such a believing relationship which does, after all, demand some kind of interpretation. Recently I have become interested in the very different approaches to this matter which are made in the Johannine and the Pauline literature of the New Testament. For the writer called John, the Spirit is characteristically thought of as subsequent to Christ, who gives us the Spirit in order to make up for his absence, as the "Comforter" of his bereaved, perhaps despairing followers. Thereafter, according to Johannine thought, one who has the Spirit has Christ in a more intimate, immediate form than was ever possible during the earthly ministry.

For St. Paul, on the other hand, the Spirit represents the inner testimony, the agreement or witnessing, of the believer to the truth that was lived out, and now is known in Christ. It means, if I may use technical language, my subjective and intersubjective appropriation of the fact that Christ is my Savior and Lord. The Spirit is my response to the reality of Christ, but even more my God-given capacity to respond to it.

Surely each interpretation suggests and requires the other for its own clarity and fullness. Whether we regard the Spirit given by Christ as compensating for and comforting us in his bodily absence, or as empowering us so that we may truly belong to him, the important fact is that we are his because he has imparted his Spirit. Neither a Comforter without real comfort—meaning, of course, a "strengthening with"—nor believing without actually belonging, will do.

Let us say, then, that the Spirit of Christ is the mode of God's presence in the Church. God's Spirit now becomes encountered and acknowledged as the Spirit of Christ, and therefore also as the spirit of Christians. It is no mere after effect or afterimage, but what Paul Tillich terms the power of the new being. It is linked to the Church, not as its place of residence so much as a kind of landfall where the human horizon is changed and the "deep things of God" begin to appear. Its function with respect to the "little flock" to whom God has promised his mighty Kingdom is that of encouraging, enlivening, and enlightening them.

We have been speaking of the Holy Spirit as "it"; we ought instead to say "he." The Spirit is not other than Christ; indeed, Jesus would not be called the Christ without the Spirit. Some may take exception to identifying what was termed above the "Spirit of Christ" with the Holy Spirit, arguing that the Church itself never made such a substitution. It is not, however, a question of substituting but of equating the two. (Here we are, back at the *filioque* again!) Unless we do equate them we are quite without specifically Christian guidance as to what makes the Holy Spirit holy.

This Spirit is like the wind which blows wherever it will. Christ is available to the Church, but invisible and uncontrollable, bending in and out of institutional or sacramental reach. He is now God's "open secret" but a secret still. He has not given up his power to any human agency, although he invites men to participate in it by faith. If we take seriously and positively this view of the relationship between the Holy Spirit and the Church we shall be bound, I think, to find ourselves in opposition to what has been advanced, until very recently at any rate, as the official Roman Catholic doctrine of the matter. This doctrine was expressed in the motto, "The

Holy Spirit is the soul of the Church." This carries the suggestion, in good Aristotelian fashion, that when the physical body of Jesus ceased to be, his soul went marching on in the Church, which may thus be considered the successor to Christ. His mission was transmitted in perpetuity, *per omnia saecula saeculorum,* to the Church as a kind of plenipotentiary with the Vicar of Christ at its head.

If this is the sense in which the Spirit is the soul of the Church, the organizing vital principle within the body of Christ, in terms borrowed from Aristotle's metaphysics, then non-Catholics must strongly disagree. The chief reason for disagreement is that there is no room given in such a conception for any confrontation of the Church by the Spirit. Christ does not, in this view, retain what P. T. Forsyth liked to call his crown rights over the Church. Has he not really signed away his power and left his deputy to rule in his place?

There are real problems in this Roman Catholic tendency to make soul out of Spirit. Actually they do not mean the same thing, whether in English, Greek, or Hebrew. Soul belongs to man; Spirit belongs to God, even when it makes its home in man. The opposite of soul is body, the visible and tangible locus of an individual human life; the opposite of spirit, as every thoughtful reader of St. Paul knows, is the flesh—meaning finite earthly life, including soul, and with or without the imputation of actual sin. This has been set forth many times with care by biblical scholars and theologians. It is therefore a bit astonishing, to say the least, that the Roman Catholic Church should choose to base its thought at such a central point upon pre-Christian, extrabiblical resources.[2]

A Protestant view of this important matter—the Orthodox must speak for themselves, and they have—would hold with Professor George Hendry that there is an abiding polarity between Christ and his Church. Indeed, this may be the very

[2] Some of the discussion on this issue is reviewed in J. Robert Nelson, *The Realm of Redemption* (London: Epworth Press, 1957), pp. 92-93.

reason for the selection of the term "spirit," or at any rate one good reason. "There am I in the midst" obviously does not mean bedded down, encased, domesticated in the Church, unless its invisible anchorage, the radical mystery of its life hid with Christ in God, is stubbornly insisted on as well. If Christ is to draw all men unto himself, to refer again to the familiar words of John, then there must be some distance between where he is and where men are, even in the Church. A Protestant would want it said that this is a distance of judgment and grace, in short, of Spirit.

It may be that this difference in outlook regarding the Spirit of Christ within the Church will turn out to be a chief stumbling block in the emerging Protestant–Roman Catholic dialogue. If the Holy Spirit is the "soul of the Church," are we to assume a succession, a transfer of power, a chain of command moving from Christ to his Church? It would seem that the Roman Church is here having its usual trouble mixing mystical and military metaphors, confusing the animating and organizing principles of the Body of Christ. A Protestant would have to make the contrasting assertion that whatever succession of power or continuity of authority the Church reveals is that of mission and of witness, initiated and ordained by the Lord of the Church. There are signs that Roman Catholic theologians are no longer unanimous on the point that the Spirit is embodied in the Church—signs for which a Protestant must give thanks.

The Holy Spirit, or Spirit of Christ, as the mode of God's presence known in the Church, is indicated precisely by those churchly events and acts which take the Church's attention away from itself and direct it to its living Lord. In saying this I do not mean to deny that the Church is an invisible as well as a visible reality; there is of course a sense in which the more the Church concentrates on the Lord's commission, the more it becomes aware of its true and essential nature. Nevertheless, the tendency to think of the Spirit as solidified and institutionalized within the visible Church is strong enough in all sectors of Christendom to demand a warning, opposing voice. Do not prayer, preaching, the sacraments, brotherly and neighborly service, the ministry itself have just this function of pointing beyond and through Church to Christ and so to God? It is a sorry perversion of their real intent when they ricochet upon themselves, become introverted, turn toward their own magnification and gratification. How easy it is to forget what a church is for!

Think of Christ's Spirit in the Church, therefore, not as a built-in feature of organized Christianity but as a permanent possibility of internal awakening and renewal. Think of the Spirit, in Catholic fashion if you will, as he who keeps the Church alive; but be on guard against the pious blasphemy which holds, or takes for granted, that the Church is what keeps the Spirit alive. To be sure, we of the Church have something to boast of, but only the Lord. We are indeed "joint heirs with Christ," but this inheritance is given us on the condition that we have his mind and do his will. Here, as always, the gift embraces and requires a task. We have a charge to keep, a preserve of memory to cherish, a hope to be won, as faith responds to grace and spirit echoes Spirit.

3

It is a hardy—some would say foolhardy—Christian theologian who is willing to take up the defense of "religion" today. Since Karl Barth, many years ago, sent his first blast in its direction, "religion" has been theologically suspect. Let "religion" stand for the complex of experiences and activities which have God as their object, however God may be defined, and one sees what Barth was driving at. All this is man's approach to God, *vom unten nach oben*, from below to above; but it has been axiomatic with Barth that no such way is open, that the only way is from God to man, *vom oben nach unten.* Hence "religion" is man's self-deceiving effort to get from God what can only be given him by God in gracious freedom. It is a pathetic and indeed tragic reversing of the true direction of faith, the standing denial of real revelation, and at bottom an idolatrous, blasphemous attempt to make God unnecessary.

This is not the place to decide the merits of Barth's case against "religion"; he himself has admitted that the case was overstated in his earliest writings. But there *is* a problem about human religiousness: does it get in the way of God or make way for God to have his way with us? Kierkegaard's sharply drawn contrast between "religion A" and "religion B" poses it most clearly. Back of the "either-or" which Kierkegaard and Barth would force upon us, however, stands another and more properly theological question: What shall we think of "religion" in the light of our faith that God has disclosed his Spirit in Christ and that Christ has bestowed that Spirit on his Church?

Ours is a time of abrupt rejoinders, overeager paradoxes, and heady antitheses, all of which masquerade as theology. Among the most influential of these is the current spate of attacks on "the establishment," "the institution," or "the organization church." Those of us whose fortunes are bound up with the ongoing religious enterprise may easily become defensive under such attacks. Our very zeal in answering their charges may give more than a hint that the ring of truth in them has come through to us. But what is most lacking in this interchange is just a modicum of genuine theological reflection and comprehension. I suggest that this missing element may be provided by a further look at the Christian doctrine of the Holy Spirit as it bears upon the problem which "religion" poses to our central faith.

Ralph Waldo Emerson, who heralded in so many ways American attitudes on this and other matters, once remarked that "first the spirit builds its house, and then the house confines the spirit." That, from one very convincing point of view, is the history of "religion" in a nutshell. It is at many points a sad, distressing history. Within historic Christianity the process of confining the Spirit is particularly obvious: the institutionalizing of ideas, the shrinking of perspectives, the very attempt to domesticate the holy and the divine—all are in evidence. The clericalizing and professionalizing of Christian ministry furnishes a telling instance of this process; so does the long effort to fix doctrine into dogma and then into creeds; and we may add to the list biblicism, the crazy-quilt of denominationalisms, and many, many more. Indeed, Emerson's dictum seems to make a lot of sense.

Yet it is so easy to become discouraged over the results that the creative intent may be quickly forgotten. True, the house confines the Spirit, but it is the Spirit which builds the house. What kind of Spirit would it be that created no house at all? Another American philosopher, William Ernest Hocking, has observed, "The house that is built is less than the house that is dreamed, but it is also more"—because, of course, it is a real and not a dream house. You can live in it, even if it has a heavy mortgage and a leaky roof; but this is the one thing you cannot do with a perfect set of blue prints or a vision of things hoped for. Is it actually, honestly possible to believe that the house of Christian religiousness is due to the creative action of God's Holy Spirit set loose in our world in Christ? That is the question which needs answering at the present time especially.

An answer in the affirmative can and should be given. We shall not thereby justify every practice, excuse every failure, in order to stiffen our backs against adverse criticism. Neither shall we wish to sit at ease in Zion without realizing the extent to which our Father's business has been left undone, his bidding disobeyed, or his vineyard uncultivated. Our involvement in "religion" is not a matter for self-gratification but for self-understanding. As with Kierkegaard more than a century ago, we must simply give an accounting of what being Christian means.

"We are Christians; we belong to Christ"—St. Augustine's statement really cannot be improved upon, as it says the one thing needful. Such belonging is hardly identical with church membership alone or with taking part in what the world is pleased to call "religious" activities and structures. But we have the structures and activities. We have "religion" in all its well-intentioned but fumbling, self-perpetuating, often God-forgetting reality. If we were to sweep this house clean of everything the critics criticize, assuming that we could, would we not simply be inviting seven other demons much worse than the one expelled? Our problem is not how to start afresh in a Utopian, antiseptic house of God. It is that of how the house may be reordered and reformed so that it is more viable, more amenable to the leading of the Spirit of Christ.

Might there not be, as Paul Sabatier suggested years ago, a religion *of* the Spirit? Is it altogether impossible that God should use even potluck suppers, mimeographs, church school curricula, and committee meetings, like the wrath of men, to praise him? No one, I trust, would wish to claim that much ado and bustle within organized "religion" is a guaranty that the Spirit is present, for merely keeping busy is a poor sign of vitality; it may only be a way of escaping fundamental issues and deeply upsetting problems. Nor can it be safely assumed that merely using the language of renewal, the dynamic language of the Spirit, as for example in a denominational directive launching a nationwide program, will ever succeed in covering up the symptoms of deadness in "religion." Once in a lecture Robert Frost said, "I should be sorry to deaden that which is so soon to die." One would indeed be sorry by such means as these to assist at the demise of "religion," which is having a hard enough time to stay alive anyway. But one might be permitted the stubborn hope that since the Spirit had a hand in building this house he will not be content to be confined in it, even if he has to rebuild it on foundations which no man can lay. *Veni Creator Spiritus!*

Such a hope, in fact, is our Christian birthright. True, we have here no continuing city; but some form of social structure with its attendant perils, some way of effecting and transmitting our "life together" in Christ, is not only right but absolutely indispensable to Christian mission and witness in the world. True, every house of God is at best no more than a "tent of meeting," a reminder that the Spirit has passed our way before and just might do so again; but some monument or memorial to what God has done in Christ, some place for invoking his Spirit, is a very present human need. Being the finite creatures we are, living in one time or space and not another, "religion" will always be indispensable to us. This is not to say that its old forms are the best or deserve to stand forever. They do not. It is to say, rather, that no abstract antithesis between the Spirit and "religion" can ever do justice to our human situation or give dependable guidance to those of us who must live and work under the searching gaze of the Spirit within the structures and functions of "religion."

In the hurry to discover and devise new forms of church and ministry, to overcome irrelevance and nostalgia in the Christian community, let us not fall victims to the old illusion that the renewing of "religion" is an engineering job. It would be a pity, would it not, if after the inner city had been reclaimed, the far-out coffee houses opened, and our pastors had become chaplains, we should have to confess, looking back on present-day "religion" with all its grievous faults and treacheries to the gospel, "Surely the Lord was in this place, and I knew it not."

There is in point of fact a coming to life in the churches of today which it is impossible to miss, and which has very little to do with program planning or a shift in power structures. This livingness is a true mark of the presence of the Spirit, after all these years and despite our repeated failures and equivocations—and we ought to thank God for it. The sign of life in our midst is unmistakable. It takes shape primarily as a readiness to be changed, an expectancy of grace, an air of waiting and listening for the Spirit. Like the Spirit himself, because it belongs to the Spirit, this eager openness cannot be pinpointed or itemized, but it can be detected and shared. Certainly long overdue changes in the patterns of Christian believing and behaving will be the result of this stirring of new life, but such changes will not be its cause.

"Religion" is neither simply bad nor simply good, but it is here because God has visited and redeemed his people. He has chosen to dwell with us and be our God. He has given us his Spirit, like the *Shekinah* of old, to enliven, encourage, and enlighten us. Our plain and palpable duty, therefore, is not that of becoming either more or less "religious," but of listening intently to what the Spirit is saying to the churches.

4

A word may be due in the final section of this chapter concerning the duty of theology with respect to the Spirit of Christ. I suppose it goes without saying that theology seeks to think about the Spirit as precisely, pertinently, and faithfully as possible; but is this enough? That is, can theology stop its work at the point where the Holy Spirit is an object of study and speech, or must theology regard itself as being, in the words of one of our best-known contemporary theologians, "the voice of the Spirit from the world above"? Does theology explain the Holy Spirit, or does the Spirit perhaps explain theology?

It would be tempting to make claims for the theological enterprise, to dignify it by association with the Spirit in a way which might seem to remove theologians from the very possibility of error. This in fact has sometimes been tried, but usually in such a manner as to make the theologian who attempts it look overpretentious and a bit ridiculous. Vocational self-inflation is seldom becoming, least of all to Christian theologians. There is really no built-in assurance that the voice of theology is the voice of God. If such a *caveat* appears gratuitous, a rapid glance at theological writing in almost any period will show how necessary this warning is. Modesty, it seems, comes hard to those of us whose stock in trade is talking about God.

But when all this, and more to the same purpose, is said, theology is still to be accounted for. It is, after all, a unique mode of employment as human affairs go generally. Theologians represent all sorts and conditions of men, and everyone probably has some theology in him; but whenever and wherever it appears as a human interest and endeavor it is bound to raise a question about its own authority and competence. Wherein lies the ground of theology's confidence in speaking so unhesitatingly of things which "eye hath not seen, nor ear heard"? By what right or by whose leave do we speak at all?

It may be that the doctrine of the Holy Spirit is not without resources for the answering of questions like these. At all events theology would seem to have an interest in understanding itself *theologically,* not merely at the verbal and conceptual but at the vocational level. In pursuing this interest, theologians can scarcely avoid encountering the Spirit of truth described in the New Testament as in some real sense the *raison d'être* of theology itself.

Yes, we do have, especially in John's Gospel and Letters, but also in the Pauline correspondence and in Luke–Acts, an arresting identification of truth with the Spirit. It is arresting because in Christian history the Spirit has not usually been associated with a concern for ordered rational statement, doctrinal elaboration, which is thought to come within the scope of theological work. The Spirit, on the other hand, has often symbolized revolt against "hard doctrine"; it has been, since the days of Paul, a kind of maverick principle accounting for ecstatic behavior, such as speaking in tongues or individual nonconformity. What possible connection can such behavior, emotional and disruptive, have with the work of theological exploration and clarification?

But it is down in the New Testament in a dozen or more places that the Holy Spirit is to be regarded as the Spirit of truth. "And I will pray the Father," Jesus tells his disciples, "and he will give you another Counselor, to be with you for ever, even the Spirit of truth, . . . he will teach you all things, and bring to your remembrance all that I have said to you" (John 14: 16, 26). This passage from the farewell discourse has reverberations throughout Christian theological history, as do others found in the Pauline correspondence. To take one example of this influence: there is the strong emphasis in the second-century theology of Alexandria upon the Spirit as the "pedagogue" who both inspires and judges all thinking in the name of Christ. To take another: there is St. Augustine's rather frequent reference to "the truth teaching within" throughout his treatises and sermons. The list might easily be lengthened. It would seem that we have, although not in fully developed form, the rudiments of a theology of the Spirit.

Let us see what can be said for such an understanding of theology. For one thing, a theology of the Spirit would need to be set in rather definite contrast with what, under Barth's influence, has taken shape as a theology of the Word. Not that Word and Spirit can be made into theoretical opposites, each claiming theological primacy, for they cannot, as has already been shown. But neither do Word and Spirit mean exactly the same thing, nor does concentration upon the one or the other yield exactly the same view of what theology entails and what it may be expected to accomplish. There are differences, some of them important. My thesis is only that excessive emphasis upon the Word of God as defining the source and the authority of Christian theology may, and in fact has, greatly foreshortened and circumscribed the range and depth of theological reflection itself. It has encouraged the view that theology is actually dogmatics, that is, explication of a content or substance of the truth of faith. That this is a fairly recent and restricted understanding of theology may not be as apparent to us as it will be to our theological descendants, but it is nevertheless a fact. A theology of the Word is always circular, revolving verbally and conceptually about a dogmatic center. Most often it is cast in the form of a theme-with-variations; or it may develop as a series of transcriptions based upon an original *kerygma*, a pretheological proclamation which it is the business of theology to elucidate.

A theology of the Spirit, on the contrary, would arise within a freer and more fluid situation. Without denying that God has bound himself to us, given us his Word, in Christ, such a theology would find within the Spirit its continuing norm and present charter. Rather than fidelity to an original positing or laying-down of God in Christ, it would aim at authenticity of utterance, the "ring of truth," within the present moment. By virtue of its working faith in the Spirit as an inward, ever present Teacher, this type of theology would be less interested in dogmatics than in what might be termed *heuristics*—that is, in making use of inherited modes of understanding—whether scriptural, creedal, or doctrinal—for the exploring and the illuminating of contemporary experience. A theology of the Spirit would be more like art than science; it would be far more concerned with "integrity" than with either systematic consistency or pseudo-biblical schematisms; and it would make its chief business the fashioning or refashioning of telling, evocative symbols for establishing rapport between the world-mind and the mind of Christ. Such a theology, again, would more readily accept its own time-bound and tentative character than one which sought to be anchored exclusively in the Word, for it would lay larger stress upon the here-and-now of theological-human existence and upon the availability of him whom John calls the Counselor.

A theology of the Spirit, for all its relative freedom, would not be utterly free-wheeling, *ad hoc* or amorphous. Resting on the confidence that God in Christ will guide us into all truth, it would lack neither criterion nor context. But its acknowledgment that "Jesus Christ has come in the flesh," namely, that the Word has once for all been spoken, is made in the assurance that the Word is being spoken still. Here the "Christian fact," the Incarnation, is foundational to the work of theological exploration and investigation. The function it fulfills is that of resource as well as norm.

As a matter of fact, it is a theology of the Spirit, far more than that which revolves about the Word, which is able to counteract the widespread *anomie* or normlessness plaguing ministers and churches today. There is no need to document the frenetic activism of the clergy, the moral confusion of the laity, or the organizational self-interest of affluent denominations. What these add up to, as the social scientists say, is a condition of general *anomie*, due in part to rootlessness and mobility, and in part also to the high incidence of personal anxiety and unreality among Christian people, as among all others. As a result we have the phenomenon of a deepening antinomianism ("forgiveness is acceptance," "no law but love", and the like) in Christian circles, coupled with the recognition that dogmatic theology is quite incapable of giving needed guidance in matters of choice, character, and social responsibility. Indeed, the failure of the theology of the Word in such respects, already noted by Reinhold Niebuhr and others, constitutes what can only be termed a great disappointment and a conspicuous lack.

What is necessary at this juncture is by no means that someone should "lay down the law" to us, but rather that the processes of decision-making in public and in private should be opened to the further guidance of the Holy Spirit. All standards are at best provisional, no matter how sanctified by common usage and expectation. Yet the Church at any particular time, and those who do their thinking in its behalf, can claim the presence of the Spirit while disclaiming any right to speak for God in matters of faith and morals. A theology of the Spirit would not be under the compulsion to bolster up its own authority but could get about its business of confronting men and women with the gospel, then enabling and equipping them to realize God's intention for their lives. The following of Christ is not made possible by an abundance of kerygmatic or dogmatic directives, but by faithful waiting upon his ever present Spirit. "No one can say 'Jesus is Lord' except by the Holy Spirit" (I Cor. 12:3).

The vocation of the theologian, therefore, is to be understood as being above all an invocation of the Spirit of truth known and given in Christ. This is an arduous as well as absorbing task. It means moving out, not gingerly but boldly, into unfamiliar and perhaps forbidding terrain. It means willing and constant exposure to the winds of God which blow wherever they will and not where we wish to feel them. And it means, as the final chapter of this book will show, engaging the world on its own ground as the place where Christ awaits and beckons us to serve him, by the power of his Spirit in our midst.

CHAPTER IV

Christ and Worship

Someone has described the early apostolic period of the Church's history as a time when "men did their thinking on their knees." In other words, theology and worship had not yet become separated. Praying and believing were one and the same. This means that in the early Church all thinking about Jesus Christ was directly inspired and informed by the ultimate value which the worshiping community had come to place upon his person and his work. Christian thinking therefore had to make room for and respond to the fact that in Christ men and women had discovered a dimension of being which evoked their utter trust and elemental wonder. They did not hesitate to honor him as Lord, Savior, King, and even God. The first Christians spoke and thought of Christ, then, in terms which their own worship-compelling encounter with him had disclosed him to be—the very wisdom and power of God, even now at work visiting and redeeming his people.

Hence it is a great mistake to suppose, as some still do, that the Church's high estimate of Christ was only a kind of afterthought indulged in by ecclesiastical theorists and self-justifiers with a flair for pure speculation. Nothing could be further from the truth. The amazed, grateful cry of the primitive community, "Jesus is Lord," set the stage and raised the standard for all subsequent Christological reflection. Scholars now tell us that practically all the early confessions had in fact a decidedly liturgical form and function. They were actions of the Church at worship which were later woven into the New Testament record, probably antedating even the collections of Jesus' sayings. Several centuries afterward these glad shouts of praise became transposed into those creedal affirmations and doctrinal statements by which the Church sought to define its settled faith.

We are concerned in this book, however, not with matters of Christian history but with the present moment in all is baffling urgency. And we should inquire whether there is still in evidence this ancient, intimate connection between our ways of worship and our thought regarding Christ. Can it be said truly that the churches of today carry on their worship in the high and heartfelt assurance that Christ matters supremely for our faith and life? Or must we honestly admit that the original linkage between corporate devotion and theological conviction has greatly slackened in our time? It does us little good to look back with admiring nostalgia to the original wholeness of theology and worship, unless there is some likelihood that it may be recovered and shared today. At all events, we can certainly profit from a serious, sustained facing of such questions as these.

1

I propose to deal with this whole matter under three headings. The first has to do with the corporate character of Christian worship; the second will attempt to delineate its sacramental nature; the third involves the question whether the "real presence" of Christ can actually be affirmed with anything like candor and clarity in contemporary, especially Protestant, worship.

Consider, first, the indisputably corporate character of any type of worship that deserves to be called "Christian." It is true that we are far more open to such an understanding of what goes on in church on Sunday morning than we were a generation ago. Then we were prone to regard worship chiefly as an experience from which individuals might gain "spiritual" benefit. We asked, and it seemed right to do so, just what we were to get out of coming to worship. And we tended to answer our own question by pointing to the desirable effects and practical outcomes which the experience was supposed to produce. In that period many books were written justifying worship as a "resource" for toughening up moral fiber, quieting emotions, or expanding the boundaries of sympathy and good will. In short, worship was generally prized as a "problem-solving" prelude to something else, something better, which it could make possible.

This stress upon the psychological after-effects of worship meant that worship was entered into for the sake of something other than worship. It always looked beyond itself; it tended to become a kind of pause in the onrushing active tempo of life; and it was accordingly valued primarily for what it led to—the incentives and motivations it was able on occasion to provide. This meant, again, that the experience of common worship was often manipulated to secure just such results. All too frequently, it came to have a *de novo*, experimental quality about it, at worst a kind of mood-music, at best a well-intentioned but much too subjective and pragmatic contrivance.

We could not have been more wrong about the true import of Christian worship. Now, thanks in part to the jostling of liturgical traditions within the ecumenical movement, and in part to the fact that our subjectivism and pragmatism, however sincere, reached a dead end, we are more ready to see that Christian worship has an intrinsic, unique kind of worth. Instead of being preliminary to further action, it is rightly understood to be itself an action, something done by God's people as a matter of solemn obligation, regular, deliberate, ordering, and above all corporate.

When Gerhard Ebeling says that worship is "The most active form of faith," he points us in this newer, and at the same time very much older, direction. It is not as if we entered into the church service as a prelude to more significant action to be taken in the "outside world," nor even as an "opening exercise" warming up the congregation for the preacher's hard-hitting sermon. Not at all; to come to worship is itself a momentous, mysterious business, and what makes it so is that it consitutes the very shape of our corporate Christian obedience in a most living and active form. Far from being a self-administered stimulus it is a God-intended response. Massey Shepherd quotes a student as saying, "Worship is the present form of God's action in Christ." That is just about as objective an understanding of the matter as we are likely to attain.

Unfortunately there are still many people in our churches who have not surrendered the older subjectivism and individualism of a so-called liberal era. They find it quite easy to slide back and forth from a view of worship as objective deed to that of subjective warm-up. Thus an overblown aestheticism bent on the "enrichment" of worship keeps odd company with the repossession of more Catholic forms of liturgical tradition. This is specially apparent in church architecture, where the "cathedral complex" dominates. How can we put an end to this unwarranted confusion? Only, I believe, by asking ourselves precisely what it is that draws and holds us together as a community of faith. Quite plainly, it is our allegiance to our common Lord. Or rather, prior to any response we can make, it is our Lord's acknowledged faithfulness to us.

Again, this emphasizes the objective nature of our worship as a corporate obedience, a shared and purposeful action. Worship is something we do because of what God has already done for us. "Salvation by faith," that principle beloved of Protestants, should be corrected into "salvation by grace through faith." We need forever to be on our guard against the slippery and false notion that by our faith we make grace happen. There is indeed a kind of Protestant magic which is every bit as reprehensible as its Roman counterpart. We do not control by means of our own faith God's merciful and abounding goodness toward us. For a right understanding of worship this means that the value and validity of this corporate enterprise lies not in our hands but in God's. We are called to worship before we come to worship, and this is why we come. Since God has come to us already in the man Christ Jesus, we must come to him. Worship is not a seeking after God, if haply we might find him; it is our common answer to God's search for us, a deed declaring that we have been found.

This calling, this "gracious calling of the Lord," is what constitutes us a people of Christ. It may, to be sure, overleap social structures to become lodged in an individual heart, and yet no man can be a Christian by himself. Our belonging to the Church is at the same time and by the same token a belonging to each other in the Church. In the words of the New Delhi Assembly of the World Council of Churches, it is only as "all in each place" respond together to the call of God in Christ that the Church becomes a fact and not a dream. This happens first in worship, because it is here and not elsewhere that our response is embodied and celebrated.

Whenever Christian worship becomes aware of its true reason for being, this sense of corporate, two-way belonging breaks through and is sustained. Then the Church becomes a reality known and felt—in hymn, prayer, Scripture, and sermon. Worship itself forbids all morbid self-concern or self-congratulation on the part of the Church, but it also stands squarely against any view which would deny the Church's genuine importance in God's purpose of salvation for the world. Rather, worship provokes a healthy awareness of the Church as "fitly framed together," an instrument taut and ready to perform the saving work of God, even as body is instrumental to the impulses of the spirit.

There is another facet to the corporate character of worship which deserves mention. It is suggested by the well-known remark of William Temple that worship is too spiritual a process to be able to dispense with the material. That puts the accent in the right place. Christian worship, whatever else it may be, is a visible, audible, public experience—that is, a deployment of material elements and physical forces. Could anything be more obvious yet more easily forgotten? Worship, in its very nature as a human event, is a standing protest against the false dichotomies by which we try to sunder spirit from matter. What takes place in it needs always to be recognized as the earthly, human, natural happening it is.

We have been learning from recent works in the field of biblical theology that it is false and wrong to set up dichotomies between spirit and matter. There is no warrant in Scripture for our strange propensity to think of spirit as nonmaterial, as wholly without physical basis or effect. In the preceding chapter we explored more fully the nature and meaning of spirit with reference to Christ. At this point we must repeat that any kind of spirit-matter dualism is theologically indefensible, insofar as it tends to make spirit seem not more but less real than matter, by separating it with sharp finality from matter. If spirit be defined as the absence of matter, and matter as the absence of spirit, an understanding of the biblical rendering of God's mighty acts in human history becomes altogether impossible to us.

Yes, worship is far too spiritual a process to dispense with the material. Instead it is the utilization and in a very real sense the consecration of the material. While Christian worship never simply identifies spirit with matter, it characteristically regards these two dimensions of being as conjoined, transparent to each other, and in constant interaction. As something done, worship engages and involves us in our creaturely existence. It consists of physical behavior, visible signs, and audible tokens. As we shall see when speaking of the sacraments, our very creaturehood requires that we should make response to God through outward actions and material things, even though that response can never be entirely bodily and external. In terms of the Lutheran formula, our worship of God becomes truly spiritual only when it is offered "in, with, and under" the corporeal elements which sign and seal God's presence to us. In short, it is just this corporeal aspect of our common worship which makes it truly and indubitably corporate as well.

This point deserves to be stressed if only because the opposite opinion is still widely accepted in Christian circles. Within the ecumenical movement especially it has become necessary frequently to call attention to the mistaken "spiritualizing" tendencies which are evidently at work in our churches. Even the verbal and visual aspects of worship may be, and often are, misunderstood as having a merely psychic or "inward" orientation in opposition to whatever is local, behavioral, or circumstantial. Thus some are fond of quoting Jesus' saying, "The true worshipers will worship the Father in spirit and in truth" (John 4:23) as if "spirit" meant mental attitude and "truth" meant psychological sincerity. A thoughtful and unbiased reading of this passage, however, cannot accept such a distorted view. Is it not altogether clear that it is Christ who is himself the truth and who gives God's Spirit to his people? And does it not therefore become equally plain that nothing short of total obedience and living trust, involving soul and body alike, is what our worship requires of us?

In worship more emphatically than elsewhere, we should become conscious of ourselves as constituting together the Body of Christ. This great Pauline image of the Church, which we have already dealt with in another connection, also has decided relevance for a right and understanding of all worship offered in the name of Christ. Two closely linked and complementary ideas are here employed to express the gist of our relationship as the Church to Christ. According to St.

Paul, we are, as Church, related to our Lord after the manner of a body related to a self—that is, both intimately and instrumentally. The image, obviously, is one that spells dependence, "belonging," incorporation. But it also leaves room for a certain over-againstness and otherness. If the Church may see itself as being not less than its Lord's body, it must not regard itself as anything more than that. The Pauline image has therefore a double function, that of encouraging and at the same time judging the members of the Church which is called the Body of Christ.

We may derive some help from philosophy in this connection. Philosophers have often had to reflect upon the "body-mind relationship" and have developed theories to account for it. Sometimes they have posed the problem in terms of parallel series of events, physical and mental, taking place simultaneously but separately. Or they have posited the primacy of one series over the other, asserting that either mentalism or materialism gives the true account of the problem. A third and generally more acceptable view regards the two series of events as interacting with each other, whether regularly or sporadically. These theories can hardly be regarded as exhaustive or exclusive, but they may be useful in showing that we do have a problem which is open to various interpretations.

Whether we find any of these theories convincing or not, the mystery of how I am bound and yet free with respect to my body will doubtless continue to be pondered by thoughtful men and women. There are certainly times when I appear to be using my body for purposes which in some fashion I impose upon it. When there is work to be done in spite of physical fatigue, for example, I force my body through a routine of behavior, no matter how loudly it may protest that it can stand nothing of the sort. Or again, there may be a consciousness of some specific goal which rallies my bodily energies and applies them to the task at hand. At such times, the body appears to be no more than a highly complicated instrument; it is something I have and use. The athlete and the ascetic, to take two very different illustrations, would seem to regard the body in just this light.

Someone in anthropology, years ago, brought into currency the idea that any tool is an extension or projection of bodily functions, the hammer being an extension of the hand, the pedal an extension of the foot, and so forth. In a real sense all technology can be conceived in this way, and the question arises whether body itself may not also be so understood. Why not regard it as an intricate system of mechanical means designed to serve, more or less effectively, the promptings of human purposes? It would then be part of my environment, albeit the nearest part, and my mode of relationship to it would be that of possession and control, however incomplete or imperfect these may seem to be at times.

But there are other occasions when I become aware of my body not as instrument, but as identical with myself. I do not merely have a body; I am my body. I know myself, and am known to others, only as being my body. A feeling of physical well-being, for example, would indicate a high degree of such immediacy of identification; then to speak of selfhood apart from embodiment would be ridiculous. Even to speak of being in my body would be inappropriate, for this would suppose a kind of bodily objectification to which every act of mere sensation gives the lie. I do not know my body as some sort of outer shell or housing within which I may be presumed to reside; rather, whatever I know, I know with my body and not simply through it or by means of it.

The French Catholic thinker Gabriel Marcel has even used the word "incarnation" to describe the way in which I participate in my own bodily existence. He also speaks of the great difficulty, in his view insurmountable, of deciding whether body is a form of having or of being. It is surely the better part of wisdom to remain undecided on this point. This whole relationship, as Marcel holds, is profoundly mysterious rather than simply problematic; we may add that it is quite ambiguous as well. While it is of such a character as to encourage careful reflection, the relation which I bear to my body forbids all premature conclusions.

The purpose of this philosophical excursion has been that of showing how St. Paul's image of the Church as the Body of Christ can be taken seriously. Whether it is mere metaphor or not—the point, as we saw earlier, is much debated by biblical scholars and theologians—this image is certainly useful in stressing both the instrumental and the intimate nature of the Church's corporateness, particularly as made manifest in worship. Just as my body constitutes my signature in the world and carries the thrust of my selfhood into the world, so the Church is analogously constituted with reference to Christ.

2

Our understanding of the corporate nature of worship carries us at once to that of its sacramental character. Indeed, it is impossible to separate the two except for purposes of orderly discussion. The mystery of the Church at worship is the mystery of intimate and instrumental incorporation into the Body of Christ. Although this may sound a bit like grandiloquent ecclesiasticism, it is actually nothing of the sort. It is a matter of Christian fact, not mere opinion. We can worship spiritedly and truly only as we become deliberately aware of an involvement with Christ which is more than voluntary association, yet never simple identity. And this profound relationship, moreover, constitutes the only ground on which a genuinely sacramental worship becomes either possible or meaningful.

George Santayana, who was by his own account only half a Christian, laid down a never-to-be-forgotten principle regarding worship when he wrote that everything natural has an ideal fulfillment, while everything ideal has a natural basis. Faith may choose slightly different words but the point is still the same. To participate in worship as a Christian means to enter into this natural-ideal web of relationship. Once again, worship is too spiritual a matter to dispense with the material.

The very meaning of a sacrament, *ex opere operato,* brings immediately into view the nature of the world in which such an action can conceivably take place. Without going so far as to delineate a "sacramental universe," must we not at least declare ourselves in favor of such an ordering of things as Santayana suggests? We must, unless we are prepared to accept the view that sacramental action is a groundless folly, that this is not the way things really are at all. A sacrament raises inevitably the question as to the kind of world in which it can be said to happen. And while we should not pretend to prove that such a world exists merely because sacraments exist, because that would be only a sort of special pleading, neither can we be content with any view which denies out of hand the reasonableness of that creaturely cherishing which is sacramental worship.

The most familiar definition of a sacrament, traditionally linked with St. Augustine, describes it as "an outward and visible sign of an inward and spiritual grace." The definition as it stands is clear and valid enough, but it has often been used in a way quite contrary to its original intention. How many times have we heard it said to mean that in the sacrament we are giving outward expression to an inward attitude! This may indeed be true, but it is not what makes a sacrament sacramental. On the contrary; a sacrament becomes such because in it God signifies in visible form his gracious bearing toward us. In terms of the old formula, it is the grace of God and not the faith of man which initiates and validates all truly sacramental worship. Not how we feel toward God but how God is disposed and acts toward us is what is signified here.

The key word, after all, is "grace," which refers quite plainly to the action of God in favoring and accepting us. And this grace, it is equally clear, is that "friendliness of God toward man," as Karl Barth now likes to call it, which is disclosed in Jesus Christ our Lord. Probably too much has been made in recent theology of grace as a sheer gratuitous and inexplicable act on the part of God. But we are not without criteria or ways of recognizing grace when it comes, provided we have what St. Paul delighted to call the mind of Christ. Indeed, faith may almost be defined, in the context of grace, as expecting the unexpected from God, as we have been taught to do in the school of Christ.

Perhaps, without merely laboring the point, this truth can be put in another way. Sacramental worship is impressive before it is expressive. It is founded upon the divine initiative, upon God's deed in Christ lovingly renewed, to which the only right response is wondering gratitude among men. Before we have anything to express we must first of all have been impressed by the outgoing and visible signs of the grace of God's own Spirit. As stimulus precedes response, as God is prior to man, so sacramental worship builds and feeds upon what God has done and does for us, and only in this light is worship something which we do for God.

Once our priorities are established there is no need or reason to deny, minimize, or discount the part played by human expressiveness in Christian worship. Certainly worship is a human and not a divine action, although it is anchored in the divine. Nothing is to be gained by ignoring or belittling this fact. Men and women bring their striving, seeking selves to worship—anxious, preoccupied, yearning, joyful as the case may be—and this leaves its mark upon everything that is spoken, heard, and performed. Prayer and praise belong to God, but they are offered by the world of human creatures. They are ours to give, with all the skill and sensitivity of which we are capable, to be sure, yet only according to our measure of faith. No one knows better than the worshiper just what that measure, that all too human measure, really is.

The relation between expressiveness and impressiveness in worship may best be seen in preaching, considered as that "audible sacrament" which St. Augustine termed it. A sermon is an act of worship before it is anything else. Moreover, it is a sacramental act, itself an outward sign of the inward grace of God. That man can speak of God at all is a great wonder, from the viewpoint of faith no less than that of radical doubt. As Gerhard Ebeling puts it, the message about God must come from God, not only because God is its content but also because God must be its origin as well. The only alternative is to suppose that preaching is a kind of hearsay or gossip which does not participate in the event it describes. The fact that some preaching is no more than this can scarcely be used to dismiss all preaching, or the possibility of true preaching. The sermon, insofar as it is the opening to us of God's Word, is by the same token a making way for that Word in our hearts.

The mystery of preaching is the mystery of sacramental worship generally—that God should make use of natural things and human events for the purposes of grace. To believe that the Word of God can shape itself into the speech of men is not, on the face of it, more amazing than to believe that the heavens declare his glory and the firmament shows forth his handiwork. Both rest solidly upon the sacramental premise. Yet preaching is misunderstood if it is regarded solely as reduplicating or parroting the Word of God spoken to men in Jesus Christ our Lord. It is no deadpan reiteration, and the preacher is no mere mouthpiece. Rather, it is proclamation of the fact that, in John Donne's phrase, "all that God sayes is spoken of me, and all that Christ suffered was suffered for me." This makes a sound and worthy sermon not alone the repetition of God's Word but response to it and reflection upon it. All the preacher's powers of expression are called into play by the impression which God's "true and lively

Word" has made upon him. Unless he reveals himself as faithful man within his sermon he cannot reveal the gracious God.

When a sermon is, as we so quaintly put it, "successful," this can only mean that its purpose of communicating God's own self-communication to men has been realized, that the impression which God makes upon us has found something like full and fitting expression. Sermon-making, therefore, is a craft employing many skills and gifts: creating an environment receptive to the truth which is to be spoken, capturing the attention, jogging the memory, prodding the conscience, appealing directly or indirectly to the emotions. There is ample room for the exercise of the preacher's creativity and virtuosity in opening up the Scriptures. It is a task requiring the evocative gifts of a poet, the interpretative gifts of an actor, the demonstrative gifts of a scientist. The sacramental character of preaching involves, nay demands, expressive fashioning in many forms and styles.

But preaching also throws much light on the meaning of sacramental worship itself, that "visible word" of which St. Augustine spoke. What does it signify that a Word intended to be heard and heeded should also be seen and handled? What, indeed, if not that nature as well as man is a theater of grace inspiring gratitude, that God's speaking is not simply a primordial utterance but a perennial showing forth which elicits in cosmos and heart alike our creaturely praise. When the philosopher Alfred North Whitehead wrote that "a dead Nature gives no reasons," he was thinking of the Newtonian scheme, modeled on the machine, in which the external world is said to consist of matter-in-motion, rigidly controlled by impersonal law. The Christian faith stands squarely against such a bleak, unsacramental view. On the contrary, it holds that nature is creation, viable and answerable to the promptings of grace, capable of receiving and responding to the mighty acts of God. Among other things, sacramental worship is the voicing of this truth of our faith that "day to day pours forth speech, and night to night declares knowledge" —that, in short, all nature declares the glory of God.

St. Augustine's mixing of the metaphors of sound and sight is therefore not to be deemed an instance of rhetorical license. By it he meant to stress the oneness of the human and natural realms before God, as well as their capacity together to express community of adoration and celebration. Sacramental worship arises in the awesome wonder that this can be so and is devoted to making it explicit and articulate.

There is a *joie de vivre* which belongs properly to Christian worship, and we ignore or neglect it only at our peril. To worship means to serve, not menially but gladly, out of the fullness of an enraptured heart. It means not only to give God his due, but even more to give ourselves in grateful loyalty to him. While it is true that we are commanded to worship, and we are rightly on our guard lest reverence should be in danger of replacing obedience, it by no means follows that this alone is why we come together to take part in this amazing action. Our self-giving is the joyous echo of God's own outpouring of himself, our sharing in his love for the world. Whenever worship lacks this high, clear note it has sorely missed its mark.

My purpose in these last few pages has been to emphasize the sacramental character of all Christian worship. There as been no thought of minimizing the importance of particular acts called sacraments, however. I would maintain that in such corporate events as baptism or the Communion service we discover the symbolic norms and patterns for everything that is done in the name of Christ. Baptism as the sacrament of initiation signifies that God does not wait to accept us until we decide to accept him, but his grace precedes and creates our faith—not the reverse. And the Lord's Supper as the sacrament of incorporation signifies that "Love's redeeming work is done"—done, but not concluded, so that God has constituted us a people to take part in it. What holds true of particular sacraments, whatever their special nuances, holds equally true of all worship. Rather than a favor which we do for God, or the sealing of an ancient bargain, worship represents the loving initiative of God toward us and the response which this awakens and nourishes within and among us.

The sacramental nature of worship is seen, further, in the fact that we cannot separate the act of God from the act of the Church. To be sure, we can distinguish them in reason and by language, and at many points we ought to try to do so. But we cannot sunder one from the other in the worshiping action itself. Using classical theological categories for the moment, let us say that *gratia preveniens* becomes in worship *gratia cooperans*, that God with his self-giving also gives us the power to give ourselves to him. His bestowal becomes our enabling, our power of co-working with him.

The Church is that community of faith which in some sense furthers and sustains the work of God in the world; just how this may be understood and carried through has concerned us in Chapter Two. At this point it will be enough to say that what God does in Christ, the Church is also engaged in doing, in its own sphere and way, according to the power that is at work in it. For while the Church must not blasphemously identify itself with God, or arrogantly claim to speak for God, it needs at the same time to recall its very reason for existence. If it is under judgment it is by God's grace that it is judged, that same grace which enables it to be the Church at all.

Hence we say, and with good warrant, that what the Church does cannot be separated from what God does in Christ. This comes to sharpest focus in the light of worship, when the Church is most consciously itself. There we become aware—at any rate, we speak, sing, and pray as though we were aware—that the deed of the Church is mysteriously yet firmly linked with God's own deed. There we know, or at least declare for all the world to hear, that God's work of seeking, serving, saving love is our work too. But how is it possible for us, as the Church, to make this astounding claim? Only, it is plain, "through Jesus Christ our Lord." This ritual phrase does not mean merely that we are going through the proper channels or invoking some magical guaranty which makes our worship automatically efficacious. It means, rather, that what we do we do by virtue of what God has done and still is doing, by his strength and not solely by our own. Thus it is Christ who holds together God's act and the Church's act, and worship is the chief token that this is so.

It therefore takes a certain boldness to approach God in worship, which Jesus in his teaching about prayer identifies with a kind of headlong, all-or-nothing importunity. Such daring is thoroughly compatible with humility; without ever taking God simply for granted, it is a venturing in confidence, an uninhibited and even impatient eagerness. "Did we in our-own strength confide, our striving would be losing." But since our confidence is anchored in Christ as "the right man on our side" no distance between God and man is too great to be bridged, as it has already been bridged by him through whom our worship is offered. If we came to God in our own strength, even the strength of our need alone, we could not come to him at all. But faith in Christ as true Word of God and Lord of man justifies while it demands our daring, trusting action.

"Christian worship adds nothing to the worship of Christ", writes William Nicholls, "but is entirely included within it."[1] To speak of the work of Christ in terms of worship may fall strangely upon some Protestant ears, long accustomed to the so-called simple gospel of one who went about doing good. But what is lacking in this much too simple version of Christianity is precisely the central thrust, the indubitable accent,

[1] *Jacob's Ladder: The Meaning of Worship* (London: Lutterworth Press, 1958), p. 17.

of the gospel itself. Christ's Lordship is nothing other than his servanthood, his self-offering, indeed, his worship.

At the heart of every sacrament there is sacrifice as well. He whose worship took him to the cross, who was obedient even unto death, is the true norm of prayer and praise offered in the Church. It is by joining our lives to his that we "make holy"—that is the literal meaning of "sacrifice"—our own very selves. As God gave himself a name in Christ, so the Church by worshiping in the same name partakes in the manward action of God.

Thus we see how sacramental in nature Christian worship is, when defined and practiced according to its proper standard. It is the very type or token of the Christian life itself, cast in the form of Christ's own service rendered to the Father. Its keynote is participation in the grace of God, made possible to us by "the wonders, wonders of his love."

3

All that has been said thus far about Christ in relation to our worship rests upon a theological assumption which must now be brought out into the open. Let us put it in terms of a question: In what sense, if any, may we believe in and practice what earlier generations were accustomed to call the "real presence"? It would seem that Christian worship as described here stands or falls with this assumption, yet its difficulties must be squarely faced.

Perhaps some members of the churches are not fully conscious of these difficulties, as they continue without hesitation to use the old language with its traditional associations. Before the Faith and Order meetings at Lund in 1952 a number of papers on the "ways of worship" used by the participating churches were circulated and studied. What was particularly interesting in these papers was the general recognition given to the real presence of Christ in otherwise divergent forms of worship. To be sure, the use of this common phrase carried problems of its own, and was not an unmixed blessing in furthering interconfessional dialogue. When one found everybody from the Society of Friends to Greek Orthodoxy willing to assert that Christ is really present in our worship, one had at least the right to ask whether such an assertion could possibly have a common meaning. Premature agreement to employ the same phrase may have been more of a hindrance than a help. But the very willingness to use it, across lines of historic cleavage and isolation, had of course a significance which was not to be discounted.

The old debates between transubstantiationists and consubstantiationists, which bulked so large in sacramental theology of the late medieval and early modern periods, are quite beside the point today. They represented alternative solutions to the problem of "real presence" which are no longer available to us. The truth is, we have ceased to believe in anything like substance, and such belief is axiomatic to the older alternatives. We have lost all metaphysical confidence in a reality underlying and outlasting change, partly because we discover no evidence of this reality and partly because our culture builds its modes of thought upon the fact of change itself. Nostalgic invocations of "the great tradition" to the contrary, our age is perforce committed to an understanding of the world and man in which dynamic categories have supplanted those of substance. Hence to base the case for "presence" upon the supposed reality of substance would be about as useless as to attribute weather changes to the arbitrary interventions of a supernatural busybody called God.

Today, therefore, when the question is raised about the real presence of Christ in our worship, we cannot expect an answer in terms of the alteration of divine into human, or of spiritual into material, substance. All this apparatus, which worked so nicely centuries ago, has to be discarded now. But may it not be possible to take a fresh look and a new approach? Perhaps our modern terms of interpersonal relationship are better suited to deal with this matter of presence than the outworn vocabulary of Scholastic controversy. May it not even be true that presence can be described only as a relationship between oneself and what is other than that self?

Contemporary existentialist philosophers have been following this clue with notable and startling results. It is my own belief that their efforts have much to tell us about the question with which we are presently concerned. Jean-Paul Sartre, for example, holds that "presence" is "an internal relation between the being which is present and the being to which it is present", a relation, moreover, which involves an "internal negation" since the fact that another is present to me means that I am no longer simply myself.[2] Sartre's definition seems less formal and redundant in view of the illustrations he gives. One is that of a man looking through a keyhole only to find that another eye is staring back at him. Presence, therefore, is never a matter of mere *thereness*, but has something emphatically to do with me; indeed, it may be said to determine me. One should not be thrown off by the fact that in Sartre's own philosophy the other is always met as an encroachment or threat, so that he can quite precisely say, "Hell is . . . other people." The point is still worth making, and heeding, that "presence" does occur and puts me on the spot before it, requiring, as Sartre says, no reference to a mystic unknowable.

Another illustration which Sartre gives is even more to the point. He tells of going to a sidewalk café to meet his friend Pierre by appointment. But when he arrives Pierre is not to be found. He scans all the tables outside, then goes inside to ask the waiters if they have seen Pierre, without success. Now he is getting a bit frantic because he had made this engagement with his friend in order to discuss something important with

[2] In *Being and Nothingness* (New York: Philosophical Library, 1956), p. 632.

him. And then Sartre makes a most intriguing observation: "It is the absence of Pierre that organizes that café for me." He goes on to remark that Pierre is thus far more present in his absence than he would have been if he had kept the date. The disturbing ache occasioned by his not being there is an experience of greater reality than that which Pierre sitting across a table could ever have produced.

Since we hear much in these days about the absent God, this illustration of Sartre may not be totally irrelevant. Do we not know God today most achingly, most poignantly, as an absence? Is not doubt actually more real than faith, so much so that faith is able to overcome doubt only by granting and including it? Our age, it seems, is in the position of Job vis-à-vis God, though without Job's claim to righteousness. We know God chiefly as an aching void, and all the paraphernalia of our religiousness can be interpreted—theologically! —as a desperate attempt to fill this unwelcome vacuum. Thus we go through motions of reassurance, make gestures of obedience, all the while fending off the mocking irony of ultimate emptiness. No wonder that psychologists and sociologists are mordantly amused.

Yet as we have seen in Sartre's illustration, absence may be one of the surer signs of presence. This is not a clever paradox designed to give comfort to doubters. It is sober and quite obvious truth. Was God less real, as presence, to Luther in his doubt than in his faith, or to Job in his despair than in his prosperity? Hardly. It makes eminent sense, therefore, to say that it is the absence of God which organizes or composes the experience of Christian worship. But that is the same as to say that God is really, not conventionally, present. Precisely because he is not an item in the object-world, he is more real than any object can ever be.

But it is with the real presence of Christ that we are here primarily concerned. It is as true to believe that God conceals himself as that he reveals himself in Christ; indeed, these beliefs come down to the same thing. His presence with us is disclosed in, with, and under his apparent absence—through that absence and because of it, as it could not otherwise be disclosed at all. Is this not the true mystery of the Incarnation, which the Church celebrates at the feast of Christmas?

For surely it is a very great wonder that God should choose to reveal himself by humbling and hiding himself, by taking flesh and making earth his home. The wonder is not that God became man—such metamorphoses were a dime a dozen in the ancient world. But incarnation is not metamorphosis. It is loving self-identification raised to the fullest power, living in the life of another, the supreme and sovereign instance of costly caring. It is at once the most secret and the most open of all the acts of God, the unique and universal act. The mystery of Christmas is not, as some would have it, that Jesus Christ is simultaneously human and divine, but that in him God moves within our life and makes it his own. It is the mystery of presence.

Christ, then, is the true *Shekinah* of God. This Hebrew word is particularly appropriate in speaking of the Incarnation because it means both "dwelling" and "glory." Thus it catches up not only the truth that God was "pleased as man with man to dwell" but also that other, still more wondrous truth that by this dwelling his glory was revealed in such wise that "all flesh shall see it together." It should be noticed, here again, that paradox does less than justice to our understanding of the Christ-event. It is no part of the Christian faith that God contradicts himself in Christ; that he is at once hidden and revealed, mortal and eternal, and so forth, expresses rather our minds' limitation in the face of ultimate mystery. Faith lives by the persuasion that absence is a mode of presence, hiddenness the means of revelation, and mortality the vehicle of eternity.

This is what Christian worship, too, is all about. But how easily it is forgotten! Understandably enough, yet also pathetically, we are constantly being tempted to put Christ on a pedestal, to revere him as a demigod, to keep his real presence from disturbing us. One can watch this insidious temptation at work in almost every sermon, hymn, or prayer that is offered. Perhaps we are afraid of presence and so incline to materialize a figure out of the past—the cherub in a crib, the kindly man of Galilee, the sad-eyed bearer of malevolence and spite. Or perhaps we yearn for something better than presence—the song of nonexistent but delectable angels, eternal verities, compensatory bliss. Our fears and longings will be bound to emerge in our worship, if only because it is we who offer it; but they must not be permitted to dictate its motives or determine its direction. Either to materialize or to spiritualize Christ in our worship is to evade his presence, to substitute the legendary or the ideal for the real.

"Where two or three are gathered together in my name, there am I in the midst." That, of course, is the *locus classicus* for any valid effort to think through this matter of the real presence. Whatever else "in the midst" may mean, it certainly does not mean "out front" or "up high." But neither does it signify some kind of diffused brooding or "mystical" hovering of the Lord above his people. My suggestion is that we regard the phrase "in the midst" as indicative of that same mode of presence-in-absence which has already been described, the kind which organizes or composes an experience. This is closely akin to that anonymous identity which links Christ with the hungry, thirsty, strange, naked, and imprisoned in the great eschatological parable of Matthew, chap. 25. "As you did it to one of the least of these my brethren, you did it to me." Here Christ stands before the believer in the very person of the sick man or the prisoner; he therefore *is* our neighbor and our brother, and this is the actual meaning of his Lordship.

If Christ is to be known in the midst of life, does this not call rather gravely into question the inveterate habit which would make Christ the object of our worship? Should we not then abandon the practice of praying to him, or of singing hymns to Christ as God, as one of the earliest accounts of primitive Christian worship reported? The answer, it seems to me, is that we ought not to make Christ more incognito than he is. If it is in the neighbor that I must see Christ, then it is Christ I see in the neighbor, and this should be capable of being confessed by a congregation gathered in his name. Indeed it must be confessed, if only to recall the Lord's people to the springs of their loyalty and obedience. Personally, I may prefer to pray through Christ rather than to him, but it is nonetheless important that I specify the source of strength wherein my confident approach to God rests. Whatever my preference, it is at least an open question whether, if I pray to God in Christ, I may not also properly pray to Christ in God.

Presence is a zone or dimension of all human existence, and the presence of Christ similarly qualifies all Christian existence. Gabriel Marcel, like Sartre, has also written much on presence in terms of his own philosophy of intersubjectivity and mystery. He calls presence a "being-with," pointing out that one may have his being only as a being-with others, whether we come to know this in experiences of hostility and rejection or in those of love and acceptance. Marcel, unlike Sartre, thinks as a Christian and makes refreshing use of some traditional doctrines without ever merely translating them.[3] Extending his thought to deal with the matter of our present concern, let us say that our Christian reason for existence, for being who we are, is Christ's own being-with us. His presence is not to be conceived as that of a hovering ghost, an elongated moral influence, or an idol warmed, clothed, and given the appearance of life by the devotion of his followers. Rather, it is the solid, palpable reality of *koinonia* and *dia-*

[3] See, especially, his Gifford Lectures, *The Mystery of Being* (London: Harviel, 1950), Vol. I. chap. 10; Vol. II. chap. 2.

konia, of fellowship-in-servanthood, which not only makes him real to us but makes us real to him.

It may be asked whether in this account of the real presence we have not lost sight of the holy, which one might expect to be taken as the *sine qua non* of all worship. That, I fear, would be to miss the point in everything that has thus far been said. The keynote of the holy in our Christian faith is not separation but disclosure. What engenders awe and stirs our sense of the numinous is not that God is high and lifted up but that he has come to us, making our life and death his own. That majesty should be revealed as lowliness, that servanthood should become the means of Lordship—these are the signs of holiness which mark God's presence as made known in Jesus Christ. And they are signs that give abundant room for the soul's journeying, across adoring distances, toward its true home.

Finally, the real presence of Christ in our worship binds the times of men together. "Lo, I am with you always"—these words are luminous with Christian meaning by virtue of their witness that Christ's presence is not confined to the present moment but goes before and after it. We are to "endure as seeing him who is invisible" because the invisible is always there for us to see. That which is past fortifies the present and opens out upon the future, by the action of the Spirit which God in Christ has given to us. Thus our very being as the Church at worship is constituted by Christ's being-with us.

CHAPTER V

Christ and Our Ministry

Why is it that the topic of this chapter should suggest at first glance a devotional meditation intended for clergymen, and not a theological exploration addressed to the whole Church? Quite possibly it is because we have only recently begun to see the ministry in theological and churchly rather than professional terms. Appeals to greater personal dedication and more obedient discipleship may have limited value in shoring up professional motivation temporarily, but they miss their mark if they are launched in a theological vacuum or aimed chiefly at those who have chosen the clerical vocation.

There is indeed a malaise from which the ordained ministry is suffering today, but this is everybody's problem in the churches. The ordained ministry has been discussed almost to death. It has been analyzed psychologically and sociologically. There has been incessant talk about the clergyman's role, image, status, and function. All this has only added to his sense of deepening vocational despair. Now, however, another kind of question, upon a genuine answer to which the ordained minister's self-understanding chiefly must depend, is being asked by all church members. This question has to do with the relationship of all Christians as ministers to Jesus Christ, "whose we are, whom also we serve."

The theological, or more properly Christological, question about the ministry takes precedence over all the other questions we are raising at the present time, because it frames the only possible perspective in which the latter questions can be answered. If we ask why the religious professional cuts less of a figure in the community than he did formerly, why he is no longer an authority-figure, why he has become more of a program-pusher and an organization-runner, and the like, we shall have to look for deeper causes than those which have been generated by rapid cultural change. Not that these latter causes are unimportant; but they are important because they carry profound theological implications and reverberations. They may shock us into realizing where our true strength lies and what our true worth is within the total design of God. Only if they fulfill this purpose can the widespread malaise under which the professional ministry languishes be finally overcome.

1

We are not without resource for arriving at an understanding of the ministry in unashamedly Christian terms. In particular, the biblical and ecumenical stresses within present-day theology have had the merit of driving us back to fundamentals in our thought if not in our behavior. We have been encouraged to look well below the surface levels of comparative ecclesiology and debates concerning orders, polities, or liturgies. Factors which were formerly called nontheological are now seen to be fraught with momentous theological density and significance. The dynamics of rapid social upheaval, population explosion and mobility, the emergence on the world scene of new nations—all have singular consequence for the tasks of theological reflection and communication. The "structures" of contemporary life can no longer be considered as beneath a theologian's notice or beyond his competence. Today as never before, and in far more than a geographical sense, "the field is the world."

These things being so, let us take a fresh look at our

present forms of the ministry in Christological perspective. In true humility we must begin by saying that the meaning of all ministry is that which is given to the Church by the deed of God in Christ. There is, theologically speaking, only one ministry. That is the costly love which God shared with mankind in the life, death, and resurrection of his Son. God's ministry to men, made everlastingly clear in Jesus, is what decides and determines ministry in the Church. There can be no other ultimate basis for our thinking, or standard for our practice, than this.

It is relatively easy to set this down in a few blunt, declarative sentences. When we say it, however, we are not only saying something that is ostensibly theological, but also something ecclesiastical, sociological, psychological, and therefore eminently practical as well. To define the ministry in terms of Christ, as indeed we must, is *ipso facto* to define it in terms of the world which God so loved that he gave his Son to us. And this is to introduce at once an immense range of possibilities, a far-reaching zone of responsibilities, which shatter any pretense to finality of statement.

Yet we must try to be as simple and straightforward as we can. Thus conceived and carried out, ministry is always, inevitably, servanthood. There is, speaking theologically, only one such ministry, God's ministry to us in Jesus Christ. Hence participation in this ministry of God in Christ is the only ministry there is or ever can be for all those who call themselves after Christ. But since this ministry is in and for the world, it has as many shapes and styles, as many gifts and fruits of the Spirit, as there are opportunities to be matched with capacities for servanthood.

What God requires of those who would join themselves to his work of love for the world is not that behavior should be modeled on some definite pattern or cut from a particular cloth. We are called to participate in Christ's ministry, not to imitate it. The difference between imitation and participation can be most important. True, the New Testament often speaks of discipleship, which means learning from a master, of obedience, which suggests an "over-under" relationship, and of following, which clearly implies the acceptance of leadership. These are all analogies drawn from the patterns normal to social life, operating between human beings in some sort of hierarchical structure. But they do not encourage, rather they forbid, that ministry should be conceived as an imitation of Christ. To take up one's cross and follow Jesus, for example, is not to set up a smaller cross alongside his greater one. It is to grasp the cruciform nature of all existence in the light which Christ has shed upon it. It is to participate in the work of cross-bearing, to identify ourselves with Christ in his costly caring for all mankind.

Our ministry, as participation in the loving deed of God made plain in Christ, needs to be quite sharply distinguished from the idea that "leadership" is what at least the professional ministry means. This is generally taken as a working assumption within the religious establishment today. But it must be said bluntly that Christian leadership is a contradiction in terms, unless it means competence or expertness in the ways of servanthood. There is, of course, such a thing as serving well, and some servants are better than others. But this is not at all what we ordinarily mean when we speak of leadership. There may be a kind of leadership implied in servanthood, but there is very little of servanthood implied in most current notions of leadership. Insofar as the professional minister exercises leadership in managing an enterprise or in manipulating opinion or behavior, he has surrendered the very possibility of being a servant in the authentic Christian sense. That this creates an actual dilemma for religious professionals in our day cannot be denied.

The servant, on the other hand, is one who has achieved a competence in caring, in living for others, in obedience and self-offering. He has learned to make others' good his own.

His life, again and again, is bent into the shape of someone else's need. He becomes poor so that others may become rich, small in order that they may be great, and weak so that they may be strong. For him, the neighbor is anyone whom he can help, to whom he can be neighborly.

Servanthood is not a tidy constellation of virtues or a package of abstract qualities to be emulated. As the total bent of a loving life, servanthood will not be easily recognizable by definable characteristics common to all instances of that particular sort of behavior. It may be smooth or angular, obliging or demanding, as the call of God addressed to concrete situations may require. Some of God's most trustworthy servants have been rough-hewn characters who did the work of love without fear or favor, letting the chips fall wherever they might, but getting on with what most needed to be done. To suppose that servanthood is always genial, amiable, or soothing in its bearing is sadly to misunderstand its real dynamic and intent. For example, Jacques Barzun once commented that much harm has been done in American education by teachers being nice to students at the wrong time. We tend to associate love with a kind of supportive, softhearted kindness, at any rate in Christian circles, which has little if anything to do with either the gospel or our life in Christ. There are ways of serving fellow men which keep their good in view and do what needs doing without displaying those overt characteristics sentimentally called "loving." This is an important point to remember.

The life-shape of servanthood, which is the very form of God's own Son, is what Christian ministry means. More than any verbal declaration can ever be, it is the *viva vox evangelii* in and for the world. Such a style of life does not come naturally to any of us, but only by the gracious empowering of the Holy Spirit. In terms of the gospel, the only sanctity that matters finally is stewardship and serviceability. There can be no eminence of soul, on Christian terms, which is not also a humbling of self to the dimensions of the cross. Instant obedience, constant self-offering, readiness to do and to be what the occasion of love at any moment requires—these are the only valid marks of servanthood or ministry in the name of Christ.

In order to grasp the full meaning of ministry as servanthood it is necessary to understand afresh the truth of the gospel that Jesus Christ is the incognito of God. The true servant does not seek his own glory, but the other's good. He is content to serve without either fear of reprisal or hope of reward. Therefore he prefers anonymity to recognition, credit, or even personal appreciation. It is not otherwise with God's work wrought for us in Christ. The very nature of that work demanded, and demands, that it should be carried on without announcing itself as such, beyond the usual circle of praise and blame; it was and must remain a largely hidden work.

Yet how quickly Christians forget this! Faith naturally needs reminders and tokens of that on which it is founded. It cannot do without expressive symbols for its own preservation and celebration. But something happens when such symbols become themselves the focus of devotion, something which may in time disable them as bearers of the very truth for which they were originally designed. A process seems to be at work wherein the self-concealment of God in Christ becomes the very opposite—his self-announced entrance into the world. God's incognito, the name he takes to make possible his redeeming work in our midst, is too readily forgotten under the impact of this process. That is why so-called religious art, with its pastel colors and pictorial surfaces, its reverential familiarity and clichéd subject matter, is seldom truly Christian art. The authentic accent of our faith is rather to be found within those "broken symbols," as Paul Tillich calls them, which are themselves congruous with the form of the Servant—those which represent, or better, suggest, the flawed and stricken Christ, the ironies of love, the tragic yet wonderful self-hiding of God.

A full and careful study of this theme of God's incognito would require the co-operation of biblical scholars, artists and art historians, systematic theologians, ethical thinkers, and others. It might call into play, for the first time in many centuries, a really meaningful conversation between faith and doubt. Certainly it would melt down old barriers between sacred and profane, and perhaps establish some new ones. It would confront us with the Christian meaning of the secular, and the profanity if not blasphemy of the religious. Indeed, this conversation and co-operation have already begun.

The radical, deepgoing consequences for Christian thought and practice of this theme are frankly shattering. What does it mean to say that God remains unknown in Christ, that he keeps his secret, that he goes in the world under an assumed name? Does this not involve us in something pretty close to sheer blasphemy? And yet if these things are not stated and understood, can we claim to have heard the gospel at all, much less lived it out? Our problem thus becomes acute and unavoidable.

By taking upon himself the form of a servant, God chooses to identify himself with something less than God, other than God, even over against God—namely, man. Moreover, he does this not alone in the single and unique instance of Jesus Christ; on the contrary, the Incarnation is precisely the sign that God identifies himself in a particular and concrete event, a given historical person, with all persons and events. He speaks and acts in Christ once for all, which clearly means out of love for the world. It is not that God prefers darkness to light, or ignorance to truth; if he did, he would not be God. But in Christ, his uniqueness of revelation becomes visible for what it is as the universality of his redemption. The very singularity of the Incarnation consists in its cosmic inclusiveness of scope and purpose.

True, this analogy of the incognito is only that, and others are needed to piece out the full truth of the gospel. There is however something indispensable and inescapable about the force of this particular analogy when it comes to grasping the meaning of servanthood. All through this pattern of acting and of being there persists "the form of one exposed to all the dubiousness, ambiguity, and darkness of an individual human existence" so that "the death on the cross is indeed only the unfolding of the incarnation."[1]

The entrance of God into the obscurity of human life is not an incognito which is to be dropped later after it has served its purpose. If God is incognito in Christ, so Christ must be incognito both in us and in the neighbor whom we are to serve. It is Christ in the neighbor whom we serve in the neighbor. It is Christ in us who makes us capable of serving the neighbor. The servant-form, God's incognito, runs all through and gives authenticity to the relationship of the Christian to Christ.

Servanthood always faces in two directions at once, or so at least it seems to do. The love of God and the love of the neighbor, taken together, constitute its meaning. But these are not two loves. Hence they belong within the one commandment in which Jesus summed up the gospel. Servanthood recognizes God as the one who must be obeyed, but knows that this obedience has to be expressed in relation to the neighbor. "When did we see thee hungry and feed thee, or thirsty and give thee drink? . . . Truly, I say to you, as you did it to one of the least of these my brethren, you did it to me" (Matt. 25: 37, 40). Only by loving my neighbor, the needy fellow human being, can I validate or make good my love for God. But this can be only because I recognize God in the incognito of the neighbor, God in Christ who makes himself my brother.

[1] Karl Barth, *The Epistle to the Philippians* (Richmond, Va.: John Knox Press, 1962), pp. 64-65.

Ministry is servanthood—participation in the loving deed of God in Christ by self-identification with the neighbor whom God's action makes my brother. It derives its strength and standard from the self-humbling, self-emptying incognito by which God moves in utter love to serve and save mankind.

2

Can the form of the servant, so essential to our ministry in the world, become also the form of the Church? Before we venture a too hasty affirmative answer, it is well to be reminded that institutional self-preservation has a way of imposing forms of its own which may be at variance, if not in positive conflict, with the form willed by the Lord of the Church. In order to serve, the Church must first of all exist. This means that it must develop structures and live by them—structures of orderly worship, self-support, transfer of authority and responsibility, historic continuity, education, and the like. That can scarcely be denied. Shall we say, then, that while the servant-form may well throw light upon our individual ministries, it cannot apply to the Church as a whole?

I do not believe that we have reason or right to say this. Surely we must agree with the words of the Ten Articles formulated by the Church in East Germany in the spring of 1963:

> The Church lives by trusting her Lord, by being obedient to his commission and by relying on his promises. Because Christ wills the Church she will remain. The Church receives the degree of freedom to live and witness granted to her officially in each particular historical setting as a gift from her Lord. . . . The Church acts in unbelief when she is anxious about safeguarding her life in the world, when she evades the sufferings which come upon her when she follows Christ. . . . She acts in disobedience when she becomes lazy, when she retreats behind church walls, or when she

contents herself to leave the responsibility, which rests all members of the Church, to certain individual persons, groups or ecclesiastical organizations only.

These brave words deserve not only our respect but our rendition. They make it entirely clear that ministry belongs to the whole Church, which lives out of freedom founded upon trust in the servant Lord, and not in anxious self-concern or disobedient shrinking from the tasks of true servanthood.

Yes, ministry belongs to the whole Church, not merely to a part or a segment of the Church. We are not called to the ministry in isolation from each other, one at a time. However personal or solitary that call may be, it comes with unmistakable overtones of historic tradition and corporate involvement. It may indeed set a man or woman against some particular tradition or at odds with a given ecclesiastical environment, but when this happens one transfers allegiance or finds oneself within another context, another memory, which also constitutes what is signified by the Church. A call to minister is by its very nature a call to serve within a ministering community. And such a community is the Church.

This is not always as apparent as it ought to be. A calling to the ministry ordinarily signifies a singling out of one particular individual for professional religious service. Thus it reaches such a person in his solitude, is conventionally supposed to involve considerable self-searching, and sets him apart permanently from his former fellow laymen in a special group termed "the ministry." It is this whole conventional understanding which is rightly being called into question today. The calling of God is first to the people of God; this is what constitutes them a people. To be sure, within that people there are raised up persons of special gifts, a variety of forms of service, who are to make their contribution to the ministry of the whole Church. Some of these, as we shall see later in this chapter, may indeed find their ministry in a professional "vocation." But the wholeness of the Church as a ministering community is what makes such specialization both possible and necessary. That is the point of primary importance.

At the present time throughout the Christian world there is a strong surge of interest in this conception of the Church and its consequences for our life and work. In Roman Catholic circles this takes the form of an emphasis upon the "lay apostolate"; in Protestant quarters the phrase which has become familiar is "the ministry of the laity." Both phrases are undoubtedly useful in redressing theological balance and in correcting the inertia which has led to an undue dominance of the clergy in our churches. Yet it should not be forgotten that when we say "laity" we are not referring to a neglected majority of church members, not even to the 99 per cent who are nonclerical. We mean the *laos* or people of God who constitute the Church in its entirety. In the authentic perspective of our faith, are we not all ministers, and hence all laymen, in God's sight? Are not the gifts and fruits of the Spirit given alike to all? Do we not all share a common obedience, a common promise?

We should be greatly in error if we thought that this worldwide emphasis upon lay ministry amounted to mere anticlericalism, a kind of "revolt of the masses" against domination by religious professionals. It may be true, indeed, that such feelings are not altogether absent. No one who has attended ecumenical gatherings can be oblivious to the small proportion of lay representatives, or to the markedly clerical tone of such meetings and their pronouncements. A revolt of the laity might not be such a bad idea, provided that it meant not the seizing of power but the sharing of responsibility. So long as we must use the word "laity" in two senses, as signifying both nonprofessional ministers within the Church and the whole Church united for ministry, let us at least refuse to lose sight of the latter meaning.

Speaking theologically, ministry and laity are synonymous and interchangeable terms. This is because the form of the servant is the form of the Church. In other words, the Church is in the world to serve. As a whole and in every part, that is its purpose. There can be no ministry for the few which is not ministry for the many. There must be specialization in servanthood, but no pre-eminence. To suppose otherwise is not to be thinking of servanthood at all.

Ministry, then, belongs to that organism of which we are members and which carries forward, however hesitantly or brokenly, the will of God for his world made known in Christ. The Church, by virtue of being a ministering community, is a community of ministers as well. It does more than to provide a mere scaffolding or framework for the work of ministry. It is itself informed and inspired by the life-shape of its servant Lord. We shall never understand the true nature of the Church if we regard it as a system of arrangements designed to facilitate ministry; far more than this, the Church *is* ministry, the bodying forth in time and space of God's unflagging, boundless concern for man.

As Jesus said about the Sabbath, the Church is made for man and not man for the Church. That does not mean that the Church has no value, no holiness of its own; it does, for God wills it. What it means, rather, is that when the Church is most itself it is least anxious about preserving its own life, that it is the visible symbol in the world of the fact that the giving of life to others is the only possession that counts before God.

When we speak thus about the Church we have in mind not so much an institutional complex as the community of faith. There may be types of ministry which the Church needs to carry on outside its own organized framework, quite apart from the normal channels and structures in which it ordinarily operates. We must admit that all too often such creative and experimental ministries do threaten institutional conservatism and self-importance. Nothing is to be gained, however, by setting Christian community against Christian institutional organization, to the detriment and dispraise of the latter. This is frequently the fashion today among impatient but deeply concerned people. The Church's work of ministry may well demand dramatic changes not alone in boards and agencies but also in the structure of local congregations. Many of us believe that this is clearly so. But this is not a plea for anti-institutionalism issued from the point of view of what can only be called Christian anarchy. Instead, it challenges the institutions of Christianity to become truly serviceable and viable to new occasions and new duties, remembering that "judgment begins at the house of God."

There are times when the Church may have to defend its very right to exist as an institution in order to fulfill its ministering purpose. The Church in East Germany provides a conspicuous and noteworthy example at the present time. However, the Church is never exempt from the requirement of honest self-criticism, nor from the necessity of being reformed and renewed in drastic, humbling obedience to its Lord. Whatever the risk and cost, that challenge to institutional stodginess or rigidity must be accepted.

"The Church exists by mission as fire exists by burning." So runs an ecumenical proverb from the younger churches of Asia. The thought here, of course, is that the Church is not in the business of storing up faith but of giving it away. It does not exist, as has been said, to apply a kind of spiritual plastic coating to the surface of contemporary life. Self-expenditure is of the essence of the Church, contrasted with the rule of shelter, safety, and survival which is frequently confused with that essence. Truman Douglass has well said:

> There is nothing in a biblical faith to suggest that institutional prosperity is a sign of faithfulness to the religion of the Cross, or that faithfulness to that religion will be rewarded with institutional prosperity. Instead, there are many intimations that when the Church models its life after the pattern given by the Son of Man it will find no place to lay its head, will be homeless, utterly ex-

posed—an organism which finds itself by the complete loss of itself.[2]

It is true that individuals are able to do many things by way of Christian ministry which institutions cannot perform. The "organization church," as it has come to be called, has built-in protective mechanisms, power-structures, a bureaucracy, and symbols of identity which admittedly die hard. Moreover, Christian action in our kind of world demands considerable centralization of authority, efficiency of operation, comprehensive coverage of many spheres of service, which only careful organization can make possible. This is not to say, however, that the Church thus organized cannot *be* the Church. Institutional serviceability is altogether indispensable to the work of individual servanthood. If ministry is not the function of the Church, how can it be that of its members severally or separately?

These things being so, we have to reckon with the possibility that God may make use even of the religious institutions of men to praise him. But in order for this to happen, much that has been exalted must be brought low and much that has been despised must be raised up. This can always be expected, even prayed for, by a Church intent and alert to the calling and re-calling of the gospel. For the purposes of ministry, whether individual or institutional in character, it is enough to know in Jeremy Taylor's words that "the providence of God hath fitted thy charity with circumstances."

We Protestants are fond of mentioning the priesthood of all believers. The phrase is rather generally used to underscore the priestly role of nonclerical church members, or the solidarity of a congregation in worship. Plainly it cannot refer to individual Christians alone, or to the laity as over against the clergy. Equally plain is its positive reference to the whole Church as "a chosen race, a royal priesthood." What is at

[2] "God's Task for the Obedient Church," *United Church Herald*, Jan. 1, 1964, p. 22.

issue here is the very meaning of priesthood itself. According to the Reformation principle, priesthood means the mutual mediation of the love of God in Christ, the sharing of all ministry done in his name. The Church's *diakonia* and *koinonia* are one. Perhaps this insight of the Reformation is only now beginning to come into its own within wide sectors of Christendom.

The fact that "priesthood" has been a red flag to Protestants for so long, that it has "smacked of Popery," is regrettable because it makes almost impossible the full and fair reading of the New Testament itself. What such a reading of the Gospels and the Epistles demands is the abandonment of partisan partiality and willingness to be instructed by whatever themes or emphases we discover. Numerous careful studies have now shown that priesthood is by no means confined to the Old Testament, and that it is indispensable for setting forth the work of Christ and Christians in the New. Here, as in all other respects, Christ comes not to destroy but to fulfill. Priesthood is no longer made a matter of lineal descent or special rank but is generalized to take in the whole New Israel or people of God called into being by Christ. Any unprejudiced interpretation must admit that this is so.

The Reformation principle does not assert that every man is his own priest and needs no other. Seen in biblical perspective as the Reformers themselves saw it, the principle is almost the exact opposite of individualism. Priesthood by its very nature is not something which a man can do for himself; it must be done for others. The work of a priest consists in mediation and intercession. He is the man in the middle, engaged on behalf of the whole community of faith in "fitting charity with circumstances." He, like his Lord, is among us as one who serves. Priesthood is not a status symbol but the plain description of a Christian's style of life. All believers share in the common priesthood of the body of Christ. To this ministry they are ordained by baptism. In both work and worship, each enhanced and undergirded by the other, this ministry is fulfilled.

This priesthood of all believers may be made more specific. What it means is the faithful performance of servanthood in all the spheres and structures of contemporary life. Is a man less Christian when he is painting a house than when he prays in church on Sunday morning? Or is a woman less Christian when she is washing clothes than when singing a hymn? These questions are rhetorical rather than real; the answer simply has to be No. The ministry of the Church does not cease to be ministry, or the Church to be the Church, when it is exercised in the places where people actually live. It is by bearing one another's burdens that we fulfill the law of Christ, and the church building or the church service is often the last place in which this burden-bearing may be done. The Church must always be on guard against interpreting its *koinonia* and *diakonia* in intramural, introverted terms, as if all that is involved is mutual help in a cozy, chummy atmosphere. There is, of course, a sense in which mercy, like judgment, begins at the house of God; but it can never end there and still be mercy.

The Church and its ministry, its priesthood, exist wherever Christians have hard choices to make, hostility to face, misunderstanding to overcome, despair to struggle with, doubts to resolve. Indeed, it may be more unmistakably the Church when its members are scattered in the world than when they are gathered for worship. The function of worship is to remind them of this fact by recalling them to the sources of their being and the ground of their obedience. But worship reaches its fruition only in those moments when the Christic life-shape materializes at the scene of action—the cup of cold water freely given, the second mile gladly walked, the real or fancied enemy forgiven. And lest this should appear to personalize the matter too much, it ought to be repeated that public no less than private sectors of relationship and responsibility need to be illumined by the shadow of the cross. Centers of power, decision-making processes or massive mechanisms of production all stand very much in need of Christian scrutiny in light of servanthood. The degree to which these can be touched and changed is the measure of the Church's ministry undertaken in the spirit of its Lord.

3

But if the ministry is thus generalized, what becomes of the religious professional? Surely some devastating questions are raised by the increasing emphasis upon the ministry of the laity, questions which may only add to the malaise in which ordained ministers find themselves presently. This is obviously not the place to make extended reference to the many studies that indicate the range and depth of this malaise, or to attempt to trace its causes. Rather, our concern is to inquire what bearing the conviction that ministry is servanthood and belongs to the whole Church really has upon the ordained minister's understanding of himself and his work. Is his vocational security threatened? Is his place in the Church devalued? Can his role, formerly so prestigious, be maintained?

The "crisis in the ministry" about which we are hearing so much is a crisis of identity. However brought about, it now concerns the selfhood of the ordained ministry in both his person and his office. In many instances, indeed, it seems to be a crisis between the person and the office. They cannot be separated and must not be confused—echoes of Chalcedon!—yet the claims of both are inescapable. Only a fully human being, a real person, is capable of meeting the contingencies and expectations of Christian servanthood. Ministry is more than an office, but it is an office all the same. I know that I am not my job, that I am more than the work I have to do; I know too that my office is greater than I am, because it calls for more of servanthood than I can find it in myself to give. So I as a person both refuse and accept my office; I am, as we say today, in something of a "bind" occasioned by what sociologists call *anomie* or normlessness. How may I be delivered from this predicament of truly agonizing dimensions?

What we are really thinking about at this point is the mystery of ordination. The word "mystery" is used advisedly, soberly, and in the fear of God. It is not intended to provide an easy way out of the predicament of the professional minister, nor to dignify the problem without answering it. But surely there is more here than meets the pragmatic eye, and any meaning which may accrue to the ordained ministry will suggest far more of truth than it can possibly contain. Every sensitive man or woman whose life work is cast in the form of the *doulos theou Christou* (servant of Christ's God) will have abundant opportunity to meditate upon the mystery of ordination.

In Roman Catholic theory and practice, ordination to the ministry or priesthood is of course a sacrament. This means that through the laying on of hands a power or virtue is transmitted by the bishop to the ordinand which places him within the apostolic lineage and authorizes him to act for the whole Church in dispensing God's grace to the faithful. In Protestantism, ordination may not always have the force of a sacrament, but it is still decidedly mysterious. Suppose that ordination may be said to mean the recognition by a church body of the fitness or readiness of a candidate for professional service, and the acceptance by the candidate of this responsibility through the taking of vows which are, as it were, his oath of office. The prayer of ordination which follows is the Church's blessing upon the ministry thus officially begun.

And yet the matter does not end here. There is still that ancient rite of the laying on of hands. What is its meaning? If we hesitate to go all the way with Roman Catholics in regarding it as the flow of power, the transmission of divine energy bestowing competence and authority, what then do we understand this action of the Church to be? Do we perhaps also believe, without admitting it openly, in ordination as a transfer of grace from Christ to us, from Church to person, in an apostolic succession? Or at what point do we stop short of this?

One thing at least we professional ministers know for certain. Ordination may impose an office but it does not radically change the person. The vocational stance of the person before the world is only part of the truth about him. What he is called upon to do defines him only partially. He is more than his ministerial functions. He is emphatically not an assortment of "roles." He cannot be factored out by a job analysis. Whatever the world may think, the ordained minister knows himself better than that.

Gabriel Marcel, writing about the mystery of personal identity, imagines a man going to a Social Security bureau to get his identity card and being asked a lot of questions about where he works, who his parents are, how many children he has, his age, hair and eye color, height and weight, and so on. But, says Marcel, all this information does not add up to an answer to the question "Who are you?" That question is strictly unanswerable because it is by its very nature inexhaustible. I know myself to be more than a bundle of physical characteristics and social functions, more even than the self I know. Part of the mystery of ordination is that God should call not merely role-players or functionaries into his service, but men and women who are always more than what they are called to be.

But there is another part to this mystery which is in contrast with the first and complementary to it. The work to which I am called through ordination is much greater than I am or can ever hope to be. If I spend my life in trying to measure up to its demands I am bound to fail. The burden of bearing others' burdens is too great for any man or woman to bear. Servanthood as the fulfilling of the law of Christ requires that we do better than our best; it strains conscience, imagination, empathy to their utmost; it is a life-shape which is far greater than any human content can completely fill. And no one knows this better than the ordained minister.

Since the ordained minister is also, in our culture, a professional one, it becomes extremely difficult to distinguish these two aspects of his life work, or to realize that they are actually in pronounced conflict with each other. Thus many of the tensions and pressures which build up within the "minister," as we persist in calling him exclusively, belong to the sphere of what he is paid to do rather than to what he is called of God to be. One well-known study, that by Samuel Blizzard, documents the fact that professional ministers spend most time in doing what they regard as least central to their ministry, namely what is covered by the somewhat grandiose word "administration," which is professionalese for "minding the store" or "doing chores". The truth is that there has been a great proliferation of duties among the clergy as they have become adapted to the peculiar conditions of American religious life, while the older functions of preaching, pastoring, and teaching have remained. So far has this gone that not a few observers of the current social scene refuse to call "the ministry" a profession at all. However that may be, there is no doubt that the clergy are increasingly subject to demands and expectations which many of them feel have little if anything to do with their ordained office.

Hence the timid and conformist members of the clergy are content to size up what is required of them and then proceed to try to fill the bill, while the rebels seek ways of escape into forms of ministry on the periphery of the religious establishment, or into secular work, where more "meaningful" types of service may be found. Evidently it does not occur to those in either group that administration may itself be ministry, perhaps even a valid form of servanthood for our particular kind of time. This thought may well disturb both the complacent and the discontented.

What really ought to occasion fear and trembling is the mystery of ordination, the holiness of our calling, which is by no means the same as cringing under the disadvantages of being known as "Reverend." We need to remain constantly on guard lest the secularization of vocation about which we complain so much in other kinds of work should dominate the clerical self-image also. There is enough real mystery, enough ground for deeply personal doubt and dread, in the knowledge that we have been chosen in all our ineptness and frailty and disobedience for doing and being what no man or woman can do or be yet must do and be if the form of the servant is truly to become the form of the Church. Servanthood embraces a willingness to assume the office of ministry in one's own person, fully aware that the person is not the office and that the office cannot be the person either.

As a professional minister I know myself to be a disobedient servant, partly because I have interests and needs which go against my office and partly also because I know, if other people do not, that I cannot simply be poured into the ministerial mold and be expected to hold this shape for life. At the same time, however, my very resistance to assuming this shape is one of the surest signs of my election to it. The more I fight it, the more surely the call is seen to come from beyond myself, the more *chosen* I know myself to be. I remain myself, my recognizable, reluctant self, even as my fellow Christians take me for another self, or if I put on a professional mask which may all too easily be confused with the self I know.

This lived tension between the office-self and the person-self in the professional ministry strongly suggests, as it deserves, a Christological interpretation. The mystery of ordination is very like the mystery of the two wills in Christ which has given such trouble to theologians through the centuries. The former seems to be a kind of analogy or echo of the latter. When our Lord says, "You have not chosen me, but I have chosen you," he is telling us something which closely links our own experience with his. At least once or twice in his earthly ministry, according to the Gospels, Jesus found himself questioning or hesitating in the face of his Father's will for his life, and in doing so he made himself still more truly our brother.

The mystery of ordination consists in this—that we have not chosen Christ but he has chosen us. To be sure, the clergyman has this in common with all Christians, yet the particular situation of his office brings it home to him with a unique force. To the one who is tempted to confuse competence in servanthood with a kind of ministerial success, as to the one who despairs of being any sort of worthy servant at all, these words of Jesus give both correction and encouragement.

The servant is not greater than his Lord. The stream cannot rise higher than its source. If there are ambiguities and liabilities which pertain to servanthood in its unique, authentic historical instance, they can be expected to appear in all further instances of participation in that servanthood. As God chose the person of the man Christ Jesus to perform his office of reconciliation and renewal, so Christ has chosen us for that same office in our turn and sphere. What I should like to suggest is that this is not merely a blown-up if rather pathetic effort to retrieve status on the part of clergymen, but a plain and sobering statement of the way things are with us. If in our vocational bafflement and distress we *act* chosen, why not say so?

But of course we also need to choose our chosenness. That may not be as rhetorical a phrase as it sounds. Pierre Maury, in speaking of the doctrine of predestination, makes the remark that it contains the whole of the gospel, and so in one very real sense it does. The reason for this is that it leads us back once more to the grace of God which is the matter, motive, and method of all ministry in the name of Christ. My ministry is something which I must accept and carry on because the initial decision does not lie with me. I do it, and yet it is done in me by God. To be singled out and set apart, as we say, is to become co-operative with grace. Whether this happens because of me or perhaps in spite of me is not so much the point.

There is much talk at the present time about tests of aptitude or fitness for the ordained ministry. It is certainly the case that some kinds of temperament and character are not well suited to the tasks of professional ministry, and we do well to detect and weed them out before they do themselves and other persons harm. The mystery of ordination, however, precludes knowing in advance that which only God can know. It is easier to say who is unfit than to say who is fit. What does fitness mean, basically, with reference to an office in which firstness means lastness and mastery of the craft means servanthood of the person? We make our provisional judgments and must keep on making them; and yet it is the grace of our Lord Jesus Christ which will always have the last and best word.

Another matter often discussed today is that of the authority of the ordained minister. Obviously he was far more authoritative formerly than he is now. He spoke for God. His people heard him reverently even when they did not hear him gladly. It is nothing short of amazing how tightly some of the clergy cling to a fancied eminence which they no longer possess in fact. They worry over this in terms of an almost proprietary relationship to "my church" and "my people." I recall a student who sought counsel because things were not going well in his parish. "These people don't want to be told," he complained.

But nobody wants to be told. Everyone wants and needs to be shown. Authority, as H. Richard Niebuhr used to say, has something to do with authorship. All authority, except God's own, is delegated; one might even call it refracted, authority. When therefore we speak about authority we speak of a relationship of derivation and dependence. It is something which by its very nature has to be conferred, to come from another and higher source. When thought of in this proper way authority means nothing more or less than authenticity. Do the words and actions of this man or woman ring true to the gospel? Do they reverberate to the reality of the servant Lord? The more the Church is able effectively to body forth in its mission and witness the form of the servant, the more it can participate in the Lordship of Christ as well.

Authority also means obligation. The word that is to be preached, the worship to be performed, the action to be taken, may not be what I would have chosen; nevertheless it has chosen me. The sense of oughtness which so fascinated Immanuel Kant is a familiar pressure—may one also say, presence?—in the ordained ministry. Seldom, however, is it oughtness in general, although it comes with the force of the "categorical imperative" which Kant described; it is invariably mediated to me in this or that concrete encounter, this or that specific perplexity. A business executive, at his wits' end, confronted by a complicated moral choice; a mother, dismayed and baffled by her inability to communicate with her daughter; a young couple preparing for the hazardous yet potentially fulfilling step of marriage—these occasions, and others like them, carry the thrust of God's call to servanthood right into the heart of the one whose ministry is sought. That God's love as made manifest in Christ should be made manifest again in the speech and behavior of the minister at just this moment—does this not mean that the minister is put on the spot and under orders, authorized to serve Christ in the neighbor by the strength of Christ which has been given him?

Again, authority means that as an ordained minister I must do what the Church does; authority is marked by what may be termed vicarious representation. Not that the professional can do another Christian person's loving for him; the ordained ministry is no substitute for the ministry of others, but it can alert them to its requirements and symbolize such ministry in a kind of visual, dramatic enactment. The ordained ministry is a standing office within the community of faith comparable to the place of Sunday with respect to the rest of the week. Sunday does not contain a single, unitary set-apartness within itself, but expresses in a regular, ordered, conspicuous way what Christians should be doing all the time. If there were no special time for demonstrating what ought to be done all the time, it would probably never be done at all. Can it be otherwise with the men and women who make up the so-called "set-apart" ministry of the Church? Their task is fundamentally the same as that of all Christians —to rejoice with those who rejoice, to weep with those who weep, to identify themselves with the incognito of Christ in every sphere of their competence and concern. But the ordained minister accomplishes his own peculiar task within this community of servants by equipping other servants for their ministry. He is *par excellence* a servant to servants. Hence it should not be wondered at that he often seeks nowadays new ways of realizing his particular ministry, whether it be a coffee-house church, an industrial or prison chaplaincy, or a lay academy. What matters is that the work of the Church may be well and truly done, that the human landscape of the world may be really changed, and that the bruised reed and the dimly burning wick of faith may be neither broken nor quenched.

To represent the whole Church in this ministry, to be a kind of stand-in for Christ, to take the place of another before God and before one's fellow men—can there be any form of ministry more deeply rewarding than this? The mystery of ordination, as endlessly creative and absorbing as it is perpetually awesome, is the central mystery of servanthood itself. Although we have this treasure in very earthen, all too human vessels, it is our right and duty to proclaim "ourselves as your servants for Jesus' sake."

CHAPTER VI

Christ and the World

"The world"—how can one hope to write anything germane or pertinent on so vast a topic in the final chapter of a book such as this? The time is long past when "world" had a definite, palpable meaning which could render it an object of reflection and discussion. Yet human speech and thought have always needed such a frame of reference, if only for the sake of remaining healthy and responsible. Some sense of the fact that we are comprehended within that which we are trying to apprehend, that there are more things in heaven and earth than any Horatio can dream or philosophize about, is what "the world" provides for us.

1

There is cause for rejoicing that this sense of the environing whole is presently being reawakened in Christian circles. Our churches, it seems, are finally losing their sectarian defensiveness in the face of what used to be called, a bit nervously but with a show of bravery, "the world." Now, especially since Bonhoeffer, one even hears appeals for Christian worldliness which would have been unthinkable during most of our cloistered existence. On almost every hand we are told that "the world" is no longer to be feared but loved, as God so loved it that he gave his Son for its redemption.

The reasons for this rather remarkable change in attitude are not far to seek. First may be mentioned the fact that progress in the ecumenical movement encourages the kind of mutual exposure and dialogue which makes sectarian shrinkage and pietistic withdrawal increasingly impossible. The ecumenical vision has to do not merely with putting together the denominational jigsaw puzzle, but far more with the true, underlying wholeness of the Church. No glimpse of the Church's unity is either clear or complete unless its universality is seen and believed as well.

Those of us who attended the Third Assembly of the World Council of Churches in New Delhi were impressed by a singular fact. Although the member churches had been called together on the basis of confessional loyalty and representation, it very soon became evident that this Assembly was in fact a congregation of peoples and nations first and of churches second, primarily concerned with what divided and united them as men rather than as church members—if indeed such a distinction could properly be made at all. This fact was highly significant because it meant the end of church-consciousness apart from world-consciousness. How could it be otherwise, when the very banners under which we gathered daily for work and worship proclaimed worldly criteria of membership—regional, racial, national or linguistic as the case might be? There we did not need to be reminded that "the world" is obviously in the Church.

A second reason for the change in outlook of the churches vis-à-vis "the world" is more explicitly theological in character. The initial stage of the ecumenical encounter was necessarily Church-centered; it involved what has come to be called "comparative ecclesiology," that is, the comparing of various confessional beliefs and practices and traditions in each other's presence, and in light of an emerging consensus regarding the nature of the Church itself. Now, however, we are standing on a further stage in ecumenical conversation which, although it may indeed have a lower voltage of delight in difference or zeal for interconfessional bridge-building, shows a definitely higher interest in grappling honestly and humbly with common issues. This new stage is indicated by Father Gregory Baum:

> The ecumenical dialogue has initiated a transformation in Christian theology. Each tradition has become aware of its own limitations imposed on it by past controversies, and hence it reaches out, by greater fidelity to the sources of revelation, to attain a more balanced and universal vision of the gospel.[1]

This means, to put the matter in the briefest possible terms, that interconfessional ecclesiology has now become the earnest of a truly ecumenical Christology.

The truth is, to be Christ-minded and world-minded are one and the same thing. What Father Baum calls "fidelity to the sources of revelation" is a potent reminder of the essential worldliness of the Church's gospel. Too frequently in the recent past the worldly structuring of the Church has been thought to be an obstacle to its mission and witness, otherwise loyal and pure. But what if the fact that the Church follows the natural and cultural groupings of mankind should mean that it thereby also follows its Lord? This, it goes without saying, does not bless any status quo but only reinforces the truth that Christ was in the world, by the power of the Incarnation, before he was ever present to the Church. What we have tended to call "our divisions" with a gesture of regret and self-pity may actually be one sign of our deepest unity in Christ. Perhaps it is by virtue of our common involvement as men-in-the-world, rather than on the basis of a conscious profession and commitment to Christian matters of behavior and belief, that we are truly one in Christ. At least this possibility ought not to be discounted, and if it is taken seriously it may lead us toward that more universal vision of the gospel which Father Baum has indicated.

Surely, at any rate, this much is becoming clear—that our

[1] In *The Ecumenist*, Oct. 1962, p. 1.

reflection upon the Church's relation to its Lord depends in the first instance upon renewed awareness of our here-and-now world in radically, not conventionally, Christian terms. Our thinking about Christ and the Church moves inevitably out of that concerning Christ in relation to the world. If the Church should ask what its charter of salvation is, or by what right it may intrude upon the world with the gospel, it must be answered that God has already intruded, that he is himself, in Karl Barth's phrase, "a missionary God." Only in this light are we permitted to consider the Church in its world-redeeming proclamation and purpose.

This is clearly borne out by our faith in the Incarnation itself. The moving in of God upon and into and through our human life is not simply an event in history, something to be remembered and acted upon by the Christian community; it is also an event in nature. The Word in becoming man becomes flesh too. Many centuries ago the Church decided wisely against the view that God in Christ joined himself only to a human mind, insisting that a true incarnation meant full participation by God in the fleshly stuff of human nature—bone and muscle, nerve endings, instinctual drives, and all the rest. If it did not mean this, God would not have become man in Christ at all, in any recognizable or intelligible sense. The Incarnation would only have been a mockery or a mirage so far as God's participation in it was concerned.

Furthermore, the Incarnation is totally misunderstood if it is thought of as the temporary insertion of a divine being into the alien order of brute nature. On the contrary, it means the entering and taking up of the processes and structures of the natural order for reasons of God's own. Hence the Christmas story does not merely record a new covenant made by God with man's will and intelligence alone; it tells of a promise of new being, made to the whole creation of which man is but a part. God enters upon the cosmic and not only the human stage; and there are present at the moment of his entrance, in type or token, all the levels of existence in the known world from the animal to the astronomical. Stars and sheep, as well as kings and shepherds, stand witness to the great event with its amazing promise.

Christ as the Word become flesh is an event within both history and nature, an event which occurs in such a way that the totality of things can never be the same again. The Incarnation leaves its indelible mark upon the world; indeed it means the recreating of the world. This remains true whether we conceive the Incarnation as God condescending or humbling himself to the orders of creation or as God taking up these orders into the fullness of his own being. Whether God stoops down, bends himself into the shape and size of man, or grasps man and lifts him up into the divine life, the Incarnation does far more than add a new fact to the totality called "world". It penetrates and charges that totality with eternal consequence. It makes the world a wholly different place in which to live.

This Christian understanding of the world has many facets and raises not a few difficulties for the so-called modern mind. Yet its essential stresses cannot be abandoned without cutting the very heart out of the gospel. If it is demythologized away in one period it will come back to haunt us in the next. What God does in Christ he does out of love for the world, that the world through him might be saved. Everything that exists, known or unknown to us, constitutes the stage on which the drama of our salvation is played out. There is no corner of the real where God's voice, his Word uttered and pledged in Christ, is not heard. The Christian way of viewing the world has not only to do with its remote beginnings or its presumably distant end, but with the here-and-now of present earthly existence. Thus the world, although it may not be an article of Christian belief, has nevertheless the character of an object and occasion of faith.

The Bible affords both text and context for this Christian

reading of the world. The same conviction that all things are marked by sin and included within the working of grace can be traced from Genesis to Revelation, in psalm, prophecy, or parable. Probably what strikes the contemporary reader with greatest force, because it is so foreign to his normal view, is the remarkable unity of man with nature which the biblical witness conveys. Here nature and man alike look up to God, lie open to his judgment and mercy, and are serviceable to his power and wisdom, all by virtue of their common creaturehood. The line between natural fact and human event is almost, if not quite, obliterated. Trees clap their hands, applauding their Creator; valleys skip like rams before him; the rising and setting of the sun reveal God's watchful, patient sovereignty; seedtime and harvest are the tokens of his vast yet awesomely tender regard for our creaturely good. The very earth trembles at the crucifixion and gives up its dead at the resurrection. This biblical and Christian vision of the world as one in God and under God is repeated with countless variations in history. The canticles and sermons of St. Francis of Assisi, the Renaissance paintings in which nature and man conspire wonderfully together to form a creative ground of praise or penitence, the later canvases of Van Gogh, the poems of William Blake are telling instances of this same yet always changing vision.

Can this vision of the unity of the world ever be recovered? Or must it remain something by turns charming and horrendous but thoroughly unbelievable? It may indeed be an open question whether our age, like the entire modern period, can take such a view with any seriousness. The cleavage between man and nature, taken to mean self and world, runs deep, so deep that each attempt to cross it only widens and darkens it. Rollo May has recently noted the danger that psychiatry and analysis will become the unintentional symptoms of what they are supposed to cure—the loss of a really human self. Erich Fromm in his protest against our "humanoid" culture says much the same thing. Perhaps science and technology are themselves products of schizophrenic forces at work in our time, bent on externalizing and manipulating everything so that nature will no longer be natural or man human. This bleak prospect has already been sullenly confirmed in more than one respect.

It was Pascal, three centuries ago, who looked out upon the physical universe in the first flush of the Copernican revolution and declared, "The eternal silence of those infinite spaces frightens me." He spoke as a scientist who had not ceased to be a Christian, but his doubt was already an important factor in his faith. Pascal's classic shudder is one which we all share, and it is not lessened but intensified by our so-called conquest of space. Man and nature, it would seem, have been driven ever more widely apart. "How many realms there are," as Pascal exclaimed, "which know us not!"

If we ask, then, whether the Christic vision of the world can be restored we are not simply inquiring whether a dead view can be resuscitated for our present benefit. The question, rather, has to do with possible hints or clues within contemporary experience, clues which may look toward the recovery of that unity which has been so generally destroyed. We are asking if the eyes of faith may be made to see again in order that the dark and broken places of our existence can be in some measure illumined and repaired by the truth of the gospel.

To be sure, this is more a matter of perspective than of propositions purporting to be Christian. No set of statments, however faithful in intention, can do more than suggest the bearing of so great and momentous a vision. The eyes of faith must do their own seeing. Yet it may not be amiss to recall to mind the basic contours of the world story told according to Christ, by way of refreshing and refocusing our insight. This we shall now attempt to do.

2

It is an interesting fact, although not so significant as is sometimes claimed by biblical theologians, that Hebrew has no one word for what we mean by "world" or "universe." The conception is there even if the word is not, if only because the creation and control of all things by God is affirmed throughout Scripture. The one and only God does not preside over a chaotic multiplicity of elements or a haphazard congeries of events; he gives unity and direction to all things as their Creator who sustains them in being and guides them toward their appointed end. But this is implied rather than stated, for the Old Testament writers were evidently more impressed by creaturely variety than by the supposition of cosmic unity. About as close as they seem to come to this latter thought is their often repeated phrase, "the heavens and the earth, and all that is in them." Whether because of the Hebrew distrust of speculation or perhaps owing to the native reticence of faith itself, we do not have within the Old Testament any explicit conception of an environing whole conveyed by a single term.

It is quite diffierent when we study the New Testament writings. There several words may be found which designate the universe. The Greek word *kosmos*, for example, appears almost two hundred times; and others such as *aion* and *oikumene* are used with a similar reference. Yet *kosmos*, though it frequently denotes the universe as a whole, is characteristically employed with such meanings as "earth," "mankind," or "people" generally. Never does the word indicate a merely physical, neutral realm into which man comes as an intruder or a stranger. Instead it suggests in strongest possible fashion that man and nature together constitute one world, flawed by sin, subject to time, and open upward to grace.

Plainly, it is Christ who makes this difference between the

Old and New Testaments. It is he who gives the world its name. In Christ, history is centered and nature is fulfilled. In him, as the Apostle Paul confesses, all things consist, hang together, make final sense. Christology may not be cosmology; it would be both unwise and unfruitful to consider it as such. However, the biblical and churchly teaching about Christ is also a way of understanding the world and world history. As Joseph Sittler has lately been reminding us, the cosmic Christ as both Word and Spirit of God needs to be reappropriated by the Christian thinking of our own day, as he was proclaimed and set forth by that of the earliest Christian generations.

The one world, seen according to Christ, does not tell a single or simple story. On the contrary it is marked by a strange, unsettling ambiguity. The world, though God's, is other than God, over against God. It is a place of darkness into which light must come from outside if it is to come at all. It is where faith is threatened and righteousness is sorely tried. It contains demonic, disguised principalities and powers which constantly attempt to lord it over man. It is where we have tribulation—care, frustration, heartache, weariness—brought on by our involvement with sin, guilt, and death. All this, and more, is underscored in the writings of the New Testament, and especially in the Gospel according to John.

Yet that same Gospel, and the whole New Testament as well, also insists that this is God's world, the continuing object of his love and purpose. This is what he sent his Son to save, in which therefore our answering faith, hope, and love are to be given. As was said at the Second Assembly of the World Council of Churches at Evanston, Ill. (1954): "Without the Gospel the world is without sense; without the world, the Gospel is without reality." This argues for a closer, more redemptive linkage between Christ and the world than words denoting opposition or enmity to God can possibly suggest. He who is—as the first chapter of Hebrews holds—the heir of all things, by whom God created the world, who upholds the universe, gives a quite different meaning to the world. Indeed, it means that the whole of things is in process of being reconciled to God, that the kingdoms of this world are becoming the Kingdom of the Lord Christ.

It would seem then that we are asked to love and to fear the world at one and the same time, with one and the same breath. No wonder that the "average" church member, who is quick to say that he is "no theologian," is confused by this ambiguity; and Scripture confuses him still further. But perhaps theologians and preachers make this entire matter more complicated, more paradoxical, than it really is. Let us see whether it cannot be stated more clearly and pointedly. There is only one world, as there is only one God. This is both a created and a fallen, hence a redeemable, world. It is called into being by God, owing its very existence to his will and purpose. It is not spun out of God's mind as a spider spins its web, nor is it merely the facade or hither side of Deity. In terms of what Karl Barth likes to call the Christian saga, God says, "Let there be," and the world is. All at once where there was nothing there is something, and from that time on there are two realities, not one—God and the world. The world, although God's, is other than God, over against God. Thus God created it, desired it, willed it.

This one world both reflects God's glory and resists his grace. Its ambiguity becomes sharper as human history begins. Since it has, so to speak, a life of its own, the world is no mere counterpart or product but a true *kosmos* or universe; yet it exists by God's leave and is marked throughout by signs of his power and goodness. The ambiguity of the world is summed up and represented in man, its topmost creature, whose self-will exerts a subtle pull away from God, dragging the world down with him, so that the created world becomes a fallen world. It is no longer the world which God intended it to be. Led by man, the summing-up of all creation, the world seeks to be a law unto itself. So far has the infection of sin spread, the estrangement from God gone, that nature too, as Paul Tillich has said, mourns for a lost good.

Hence the world, on Christian terms, is neither simply a good thing nor only a bad thing, but a good thing spoiled. It is the ground both of man's misery without God and of his greatness with God. It is the locus or environment of man's responsibility, the testing place of his God-given yet self-distorted freedom. The promise or frustration of the world is focused in man's relationship to God. In acting either with or against God, he acts for the whole creation, whose standing representative he is, "swinging between Hell-gate and Heaven-gate."

The world therefore is never merely neutral, never a random assortment of bare facts, but always humanly ambiguous, heavy with both peril and promise for man. That is the one and only world in which we have to live. Although it has not lost completely all traces of a "dearest freshness deep down things" which belongs to it as God's good creation, the world has acquired a density, a recalcitrance, which gives it the character of enmity toward God. Thus the world, including man, bears the double aspect of life and death in such a mixed and baffling way that one is easily taken for the other.

This reading of the world in the light of Christ is really not so difficult, and there are other ways of understanding it than that of sheer antithesis or the posing of dialectical alternatives. Also, it is more pertinent to our contemporary experience and situation than we usually acknowledge. Technology, for instance, has blurred and not sharpened the distinction so overdrawn in modern life between what is natural and what is human. It has long since become impossible to think of a wholly neutral physical universe, as Newton did, composed of soundless, mindless, scurrying factuality pure and simple. The discovery and application of nuclear fission have seen to that. Neither does it make any kind of sense to keep on asserting the lonely, lordly independence of man against whatever is thought to be impersonal or subhuman. The truth is that man has been victimized by his own productions so that he no longer knows who he is before God. The question asked in Eden, "Adam, where are you?" is asked again today with mounting emphasis and gravity. All this has been rehearsed many times from many points of view. We are more vulnerable to the truth of Scripture and the gospel than we have been for centuries.

But old prejudices die hard. At this point someone is bound to ask whether science and its so-called results can be so jauntily dismissed. Surely it is premised upon the very duality between man and his world which the Christian faith seems to call in question. On the terms laid down by science, man is subject, the world is object. This is to say that the world is nature, neither more nor less, which means in Percy Bridgman's phrase "the way things are" in contrast to what we wish or fear them to be. Accordingly, it is generally supposed that science objectifies or externalizes whereas faith internalizes or subjectivizes. Any presumed concordat reached between these two modes of explanation and interpretation can only be a shaky, inconclusive truce.

What is forgotten in this way of putting the problem is that science is not only a battery of methods or a body of data but a manner of approach, a human community of inquiry and intellectual exhange, indeed a fundamental style of life. Forgotten as well is that Christian faith is not restricted to something vague and evanescent called the soul, but has to do with "all things" in their many-dimensioned reality. Both faith and science are at grips with truth in its demanding, elusive wholeness. From this viewpoint one can almost, if not quite, agree with the remark attributed to Reinhold Niebuhr that whereas science tells a lot of little truths on behalf of a great big lie, Christian faith tells a lot of little lies on behalf of a great big truth.

It must therefore be concluded that science and faith do not embrace two different worlds, but one admittedly ambiguous world. This does not mean that we can give sweeping theological answers to properly scientific questions, or that the invention of some new formula can send faith packing once for all. Instead, we ought to be able to agree that common ground may be cleared, that fragmentation of truth must be resisted, that science and faith have a great deal to say to each other. What, in conscience or reason, prevents us from realizing that although we may use different languages we are referring to one world in which what is indicated by the abstract terms "man" and "nature" coexist and coincide? This may not solve all difficulties overnight, but it will certainly provide a healthier climate for significant conversation.

If scientists should hesitate to make this affirmation of a common ground of truth, Christian believers, on the other hand, can scarcely avoid making it. Within the perspective afforded by our faith, the human and the natural have their meaning only in the terms set by each other. This, as we have seen, is because the world disclosed to faith is one, reflecting however brokenly or dimly its beginning, continuance, and ending in God. In other words, the unity of the world is not inherently its own but given, that is, purposed and bestowed through a relationship as primordial as it is ultimate. In this perspective, nature is no mere backdrop to the engrossing drama of human sin and salvation, and man is neither an absurdity nor an excrescence with respect to the passage of natural facts and forms.

Yet the unity of the world is obscure and not obvious even to the eyes of faith. Here unity means precisely ambiguity, for to repeat, the world is both the proving ground and the violation of "the Love which moves the sun and the other stars." Thus there can be no simple affirmation of the world which does not at the same time require its negation. But this ought not to be viewed in Stoic fashion as refusal to become involved, or as a call to skeptical suspension of belief altogether. As I have written elsewhere:

> The deeper Christian truth about the world is that, in spite of the principalities and powers which lord it over men, the world still belongs to God; far from being merely a neutral realm, it is the realm in which response to God must be made, in which it is strictly impossible for man to be neutral toward God.[2]

The Christian framework for an understanding of the world commends itself, therefore, with striking relevance to men and women of our time and place. We know today, as the modern age has never known before, that nature is not impervious to our suffering and striving, but viable to human sin and vulnerable to cosmic evil. Nature today is as much threatened by damnation as man has ever been; like man, it groans for redemption and release. Millions of people have more than a premonition that this is so. We also know far better than our forebears that man is not only *ego* but *id*, a creature of circumstance and the unconscious, the most natural thing in the world. The fallen and the redeemable world are one; and from faith's point of view this is perhaps a mark of very fortunate ambiguity indeed.

3

Into this world, this "God-haunted house," the Lord and Father of mankind sends his own Son to save us. There is a certain pathos in his coming, for although expected he does not come as expected, so that in him God is as much hidden as he is revealed. From the outset shame and glory, human reality and divine mystery, servanthood and Lordship are strangely knit together in his life. His presence attracts some and repels others. His message both accommodates itself to the minds of men and stretches them to the breaking point. In

[2] *New Frontiers of Christianity* (New York: Association Press, 1962), p. 249.

his person and work he flashes no credentials, flourishes no signature of divine authority, yet he acts in the world with an otherness that is unmistakable. He invites all, but coerces none. He leaves men free to choose, as they were before he came.

Nevertheless, with the advent of God in Christ the situation of man-in-the-world has utterly changed. It is not simply that an additional option has appeared, or even that a fuller truth has been declared and demonstrated, but that a new kind of being has become entirely possible and a new age has been ushered in by this amazing act of God on our behalf. Small wonder that the new community called forth by this event was radically persuaded that if it had such cosmic reverberations it must also have had cosmic reasons. The Lord of the new faith was no mere founder of one more religion, but the Lord and the light of the world.

It is of course this same profound conviction which later made the doctrine of the Trinity essential to the thinking of the Church. He who was enmanned in Jesus of Nazareth was most assuredly the Word by whom all things were made in the beginning. Only the God who creates can recreate the world. Now history stops repeating itself and tells a different story. It is the Father who brings the world into being by the call of his Word through the work of his Spirit; and it is likewise the Father who moves to save that world, estranged and bent away from him in sin, by the same Word now manifest as his Son through the communion of the same Holy Spirit. Far from introducing nice distinctions into Deity or bringing a kind of higher arithmetic into the service of theology, the doctrine of the Trinity is monotheism revised and enlarged; it affirms, as we saw earlier, the unity of God as Maker and Redeemer, expressing the central, crucial truth that Jesus Christ is indeed the world's Lord and Savior.

Another way of putting this conviction, which has been hinted at before, is to say that what God does in Jesus Christ is an eventful action both unique and universal. It will not do to stress the singular, specific nature of God's loving deed in Christ so that its dimensions of awesome magnitude and distance tend to drop almost completely out of sight. Some current protests against "universalism" in theology fall utterly wide of the mark because they appear to imply, without ever coming right out and stating it, that the only true alternative is an exclusivism which is no part of the gospel. But neither will it do to emphasize the cosmic universality of the Christ-deed of God so that it loses all semblance of revelatory disclosure, becoming just another word for general providence. Since it is truly God who acts, "all things" are caught up and absorbed into his action. But since it is in Christ he acts, one point in time and space and not another must become the vantage point and standing point for seeing just how universal in its reach and grasp God's action really is. St. Paul may not have been a method-conscious, systematic theologian, as biblical scholars keep reminding us; but his assertion that in Christ all things consist or hang together is a notable historic instance of the balance which theology must always strike between uniqueness and universality in its reading of the truth of faith.

Still another way of coming at this point of focal significance is to say that God in Christ acts for all men precisely by acting in one man. Jesus as servant Lord takes to himself, and so up into God, the very substance of what it means to be human. Just because he is one individual man and not another, all humankind is represented and incorporated in him. This is what Irenaeus endeavored to make clear in his teaching that the Incarnation and redemption in Christ constitute the recapitulation or summing-up of universal history. Representative man by very definition cannot be man-in-general. Whatever else a man may be, he is not an abstract noun. In the human realm, what is common is the most singular and peculiar; its *sine qua non* is personhood or selfhood. Adam may indeed be transcended in Christ, but he must be there in order to be transcended. The Gospel wisely hesitates to say that God became a man in Jesus, but prefers to say that he became man, that his Word became flesh and dwelt among us, full of grace and truth. This does not mean that the humanity of Jesus was a generalized or impersonal one, for that would be a contradiction in terms. But it does mean that by the power of God in him, Jesus' manhood, in a favorite phrase of Irenaeus', is a "leaven" acting within all humanity. He is not so much a fair sample of the whole as he is the "first fruits" or "new Adam" or "pioneer and perfecter" of the human species. Christ does far more than pinpoint or localize God's revealing and redeeming love; he energizes it by embodying it, gives it away, and sets it loose in the world once for all. What God does in him for man, he does within man and not upon man.

Thus God in Christ is doing an utterly new thing. He is not adding a new religion to the bewildering array of old ones; rather, what he does constitutes the end of mere religion and the ushering-in of the radical possibility of faith. The novelty of this eventful deed consists in its complete reversal of direction—the way of man toward God crumbles before God's approach and entrance into man. The old is not discarded or negated; it does not have to be, because it is fulfilled. Righteousness has been swallowed up in forgiveness. Christ by being made sin has broken its tyranny, by assuming guilt has absorbed its sting, by dying has killed death. Now we live in another sort of world altogether, whether we know and like it or not.

The newness of the gospel is of a piece with its goodness. For it tells us of a God who is disclosed in our questions even more than in our answers, in our fears as well as our hopes, in our weakness rather than in our strength. It tells us, not what we must do to commend ourselves to God, but what God has already done and is doing still to commend himself to us. He has sweated it out among us, seen it through, gone with us to the end. Since he who has acted thus in Christ is indeed God, our human situation in the world is forever different. The world itself is different. It has been entered and irradiated by grace and truth so that even in its turbulence and heartache there may be discovered real peace and lasting joy.

Our Christian faith does not possess God's deed-of-gift in Christ as something to be made available to the world through its own missionary generosity. No, the deed has already been done, the gift already given. It is not as though we had to get the world to listen to us, to bring the good news across some no-man's-land to enemy territory. The dayspring from on high has already visited us and is lodged within the world. Old things have become new, the rough places made plain; God has humbled the high and exalted the low; henceforth it is a matter of seeing and doing the truth which has been vouchsafed to us.

One thing we know: wherever we may be called upon to go in the world, whatever we may have to face, God has been there already in the servant-form of Christ. His co-humanity with us is the ground of our hope for the restoration of the human. This must be understood not abstractly but concretely. Christ meets us not as a hovering ghost but as a living presence in our midst, incognito yet incarnated in "the least of these" our neighbors and brothers. To be human, as Masao Takenaka comments, means to be a man between men; that is the significance of Christ's humanity and ours. As Professor Takenaka continues, "We recognize that there is a big difference between Abraham and us. Abraham went out on his journey without knowing where to go. We also go out into the world without knowing about many things. But one thing we know: the living Christ is already there among men in the world where we go."[3]

Since Christ is there already wherever we turn in the world,

[3] *Laity*, Nov., 1963 (World Council of Churches, Geneva), p. 24.

it is not the task of faith to bring him to the world as if he were not otherwise available. Instead, it is faith's genius to bring the Christ that lives in the neighbor and the brother up to the level of visibility. It is of course only because Christ has identified himself with all men in their need that we are emboldened to identify them with Christ. But since this *is* the meaning of God's deed in him, we may and must make this identification. Not that I should serve my neighbor as a stepping-stone to divine approval, for this would be to use my neighbor, not to love him. Yet when I see my neighbor I see more than a needy fellow human being, though never less; I see and serve my Lord in him, not as an inference or implication but as a presence.

Something like this is what Paul Van Buren calls the secular meaning of the gospel. There is a way of viewing the world and of acting in it which is not "religious" just because it is authentically Christian. It has tremendous consequences for "religion" since it involves the transvaluing of all our accustomed values, priorities, and expectations, but it does not take place solely or even chiefly within the religious order. If in Christ God is engaged in nothing less than reconciling the world to himself, then it is in the whole world and not in some chosen segment of it that participation in God's saving action must occur. Indeed the gospel, taken with the seriousness which it deserves, makes short work of any distinctions we might like to draw between the secular and the religious. The secular is sacred, claimed for God by the suffering and serving Lordship of Christ.

4

As this book draws to a close, what more shall we say concerning the life of Christians in the world God gave his Son to save? The answer does not lie in making a list of desirable virtues appropriate for us to exemplify if we could. Neither does it consist in cataloguing commandments or their corresponding duties. Types of goodness and oughtness do assuredly characterize the life in Christ, but these cannot begin to define it in its flexible fullness.

How then shall this question be faced and met? It is becoming customary nowadays to say that a Christian's life is not a religious but a worldly one. With this view I, for one, have no wish to quarrel, but I think we might be more assiduous in asking what it really means. Christian worldliness is already in danger of becoming just another slogan in the churches' campaign of self-advancement, when it ought instead to point toward a profound revision of those patterns of thought and action which have all too often blunted the edge of responsible Christian witness and mission in and for the world.

Surely what God requires of us is that we share his own love for the world made everlastingly plain in Jesus Christ. That means this altogether contemporary world of rising national and racial expectations, of population explosions, of vast and terrifying group tensions and power conflicts, of personal disruption and cultural chaos. The salvation promised by the gospel does not mean being snatched from the world, and certainly it is not a better adjustment to the world; it is a coming-to-life, a being-made-new which takes place in and yet is not wholly of this world. However, we always need to be reminded that in order to be not of the world we have first of all got to be in it. Christian worldliness provides this greatly needed reminder.

When Reuel Howe suggests that in the rite of confirmation Christians "join the world," not insensitively or irresponsibly but as voluntary, knowing participants in its life and work, he is pointing in the same direction. There is no escape from the world this side of death, not even a Christian escape; and therefore it is better to explore and embrace the world, in all its ambiguous potentiality for good or ill, than to shun or try to rise above it. True, there is no iron-clad guarantee that such a course will "succeed," because the gospel does not measure discipleship in these terms. Suffering is far more likely to be our portion. In that way and not another we may be assured that we are taking part in the very work of Christ.

Christian worldliness is frequently and badly misunderstood. It does not mean a limping, Johnny-come-lately sophistication, nor a studied, calculated casualness toward events and persons, nor again a sheer delight in everything secular and profane. To be sure, the style of life to which these words point is one that is alert and knowledgeable with respect to worldly realities and possibilities; it also has a stubborn, healthy regard for the bewildering diversity and complexity of experience, for what Whitehead calls "the multifariousness of the world—the fairies dance, and Christ is nailed to the cross." But meeting the world on its own ground need not involve taking the world at its own terms. One whose life is truly hid with Christ in God sees more in the world than lies on its circumstantial surface. His vision of the world is, after all, *sub specie aeternitatis*, or if that is to claim too much, at least *sub specie Christi*, informed by the presence of Christ.

To love the world as God in Christ loves it is to accept the world, its processes and structures, its spaces and times made known or to be made known to us, as man's God-given opportunity for faith. That suffering will be involved in this acceptance is a foregone conclusion. There can be no giving of self to others, no submitting to the conditions which things themselves set for us, which is exempt from the risk of pain, frustration, or loss. The servant is not above his servant Lord. Although we may agree with Robert Frost that "Earth's the right place for love, I don't know where it's likely to go better," we are not thereby excused from facing the fact that love sometimes goes wrong in the world, because the world is not yet ready for its ministries and testimonies. Nevertheless it is necessary to stay with Christ in his suffering, to add our wounds to his, as Pascal wrote, if that which is accepted is also to be reconciled to God.

Christian worldliness is a way of both understanding and acting in the world. Indeed, it means that understanding becomes action; faith is completed in love—love which is both a seeing and a doing of the truth disclosed by God in Christ. For such love the world provides its ever changing context; more than a frame of reference, it is allowed to "write the agenda," to shape the responses, and to direct the intention of the worldly Christian as he seizes the opportunities and occasions for faithful love which are presented to him.

This juxtaposing of the words "Christian" and "worldly" will undoubtedly produce a shock in many minds, if only because it involves such a wrenching of traditional stereotypes of pietism and moralism nourished by the churches. This shock, however, may be a wholly salutary one. The shades of John Bunyan and Jeremy Taylor will simply have to be displeased. Their metaphors of pilgrimage and warfare for rendering the Christian's manner of life still ring true and have much to commend them, but their uneasy, world-avoiding search after personal "holiness" is not for us. It will not do to go on offering false allegorical alternatives and counterfeit crucifixions to men in the name of Christ. There is enough real pain in the world, enough real loss and defeat at one another's hands, without adding any more. Why should the word "Christian" always seem to carry a narrowing, restricting meaning? As Ian Fraser writes, "The Christian life is a full-bodied one. . . . Don't forget the steward has his rations, his sex life, his night out. His Lord wills it so."[4]

The stewardship which is so large a part of Christian worldliness as here described may also be called a vocation of imaginative responsibility. Pretty generally, the human imagination has not been thought of as having moral importance; but it is futile to assume responsibility where not even an

[4] *Ibid.*, p. 11.

imagined relationship exists. When Jesus was asked, "Who is my neighbor?" he answered not with a definition but with a story, an imaginative illustration. Is it not through works of imagination that our moral sensibilities are most often awakened or enlarged? Just as in the Bible, where parable and prophecy are no strangers to each other, so in the novels of Dickens or Camus, the drawings of Daumier or Kathe Köllwitz, we are shown most powerfully who our neighbor is, and what love has to contend with in the world.

The reason the arts have lately come so much into the focus of theological attention is that they are indispensable for reinvigorating the Christian imagination, whose powers have so long lain dormant or been regarded as supect, as it bears upon thc tasks of living responsibly in the world. It is perhaps not to be wondered at that the Christ-figure assumes so many incognitos in contemporary art forms, quite outside the normal channels of conventional religious expression. Shapes that are externally secular but internally significant for Christian reflection and action are encountered in all the arts. In ways as compelling as they are various they body forth the open secret of God. If love, as Bishop Charles Gore once said, is the ability "to read statistics with compassion," then the office of the arts in nurturing the responsible imagination becomes of the utmost importance.

This function of the arts should not be misunderstood. The relationship between art and morality, or social responsibility, is complicated and perhaps is a perennially open question. Art has clearly more to do with disclosure of the real than with decision for the good. Yet the wholeness of the world under God forbids that art should be completely severed from the other concerns and endeavors of man. So, in the contemporary arts especially, there is a very considerable amount of documentation and appraisal regarding man's condition in the prcsent world; by and large the arts of our time constitute a standing and by no means ineffective protest against the widespread mechanization and dehumanization of life, and therefore have profound reverberations in the moral realm. Through the arts, therefore, we are enabled more surely to "join the world" and so to act responsibly as Christian men and women in it. Before we have the right to speak to the world it is required that we listen to what the world is trying to say to us. There is no better way than that provided by the contemporary arts.

Again, Christian worldliness is almost a contradiction in terms, because it is not, as the phrase suggests, a particular set of traits or attitudes that can be distinguished and commended as being Christian; rather, it signifies various ways of getting lost in the world, controlled only by the costly, incognito caring which is the mind of Christ. The accent of such a life-style as this phrase has in view is forever upon the world that is being saved, that groans for redemption, and not upon the quality of our response to it. Another way of saying this is that Christian worldliness cares far more about being human and humane than about being or remaining Christian. That caring is in fact a kind of carelessness so far as distinctiveness or definability goes. Such careless caring, oddly enough, is the most Christian thing about it; all it asks for itself is that it may be used by God, in D. H. Lawrence's words, "as the thin edge of the wedge."

We are not, of course, entirely without marks or signals of the presence of this kind of worldliness in the world. "We are Christians; we belong to Christ." As we know ourselves to be children of God, at home in his world, we also know our sonship, our at-homeness, as enmanned and going before us in him who is both Word of God and Lord of man. The form of Christ is waiting in the world to be formed in us. Many men and women who bear the name of Christ will shrink from such all-or-nothing identification with the world that God loves. But there will be others, led by the Holy Spirit, who will join themselves to the Son of man in his worldly incognito assumed for our sakes. They will not be afraid of getting lost in order that others may be found. Like Christ himself, they may be able to save others but not themselves. They will become those humble and obedient servants through whose weakness we are made strong and by whose faith we are made whole. And God himself will be their God, and ours.